Become the CEO of You, Inc.

Become the CEO of You, Inc.

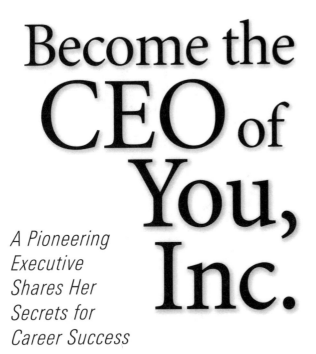

A Pioneering Executive Shares Her Secrets for Career Success

Susan Bulkeley Butler

PARIBUS PRESS

New Canaan, Connecticut

Published by
Paribus Publishing Ltd.
161 Cherry Street, New Canaan, CT
www.ParibusPress.com

Copyright © 2006 by Susan Bulkeley Butler
www.SBBInstitute.org

ISBN 1-933705-00-0

Printed in the United States of America

DEDICATION

To all of my current and future mentees and your career successes, and to my American Airlines seatmate who has always believed in me and helped me to achieve my dreams.

"The future belongs to those who believe in the beauty of their dreams."

—ELEANOR ROOSEVELT

CONTENTS

PREFACE

You are holding in your hands an exceptional book by an exceptional woman. The story of what makes this book exceptional can be told through the story of what makes its author exceptional.

As the first woman professional at a then–Big 8 accounting firm, Susan Bulkeley Butler learned the vital importance of having a mentor, and she credits her mentors' support for her having made history as the first woman partner of Accenture. Over the course of more than three decades with this now over-$15 billion global management consulting, technology services, and outsourcing company, which she capped off in the Office of the CEO as the right hand to its chairman, she perfected the art of being a mentor.

Susan has served as a mentor to countless of Accenture's 123,000 employees as her career sent her crisscrossing the globe. Her work included managing the Philadelphia office, and some of the world's largest organizations were among her clients. In spite of the demands of her career, she championed hundreds (if not thousands) of associates to become managers and managers to become partners.

Just as importantly, outside the office she took on both a formal and informal mentoring role with as many or more outstanding men and especially women she encountered through her extensive community leadership positions, reflecting her broad interests in everything from government to the Girl Scouts to JA Worldwide (formerly Junior Achievement).

Through her tireless mentoring efforts, Susan has come to coach more people than perhaps anyone else I've ever personally known. I've been awed by her selfless desire to "give forward" by nurturing the next generation of women leaders.

And while others give "lip service" to being of service, Susan truly walks her talk. Whereas some merely point out the need for more women to enter the ranks of academia in the fields of math, science, and technology, Susan actually stepped up to the plate and endowed an Operations Management professorship for a woman in the Krannert School of Management at her alma mater, Purdue University.

Upon her "retirement" (if you can call it that. I've never met a busier "retired" person!), Susan founded the Susan Bulkeley Butler Institute for the Development of Women Leaders to put into action the ideas she generated over a lifetime of helping women develop leadership skills. I've witnessed firsthand the excitement in rooms full of collegiate women who were thrilled that an executive of Susan's stature was taking the time to address them and answer their questions.

I've learned more from Susan than perhaps any other executive I've ever encountered. In some ways, we're very much alike. Although we are a couple of decades apart in age, we both grew up in the Midwest (where people do crazy things like go to church on Sundays and vote on Election Day), and we were both very active in Girl Scouts. Thereafter, we both went on to universities in the Midwest, followed by careers in business. When we first crossed paths in the early 1990s, it was because our shared commitment to the mission of mobilizing capital to women business owners led us both to serve as cofounders of a not-for-profit organization with this objective started by our mutual friend Susan Davis (founder of the Committee of 200) called the Capital Circle.

But in other ways, I have learned the most from our differences. After careers on Wall Street, in strategy consulting, and in media management, I opted to start my own firm and to devote myself to writing books. I respected how Susan, too, constantly tapped different strengths, reinventing herself yet devoting more than thirty years to a single company. She became a driving force behind the change management practice of one of the world's largest organizations and learned a great deal about how to work with people to accomplish massive change.

I was fascinated to learn several years ago about Susan's four-part approach to managing change, which she used with her clients and her career. I immediately started to apply that approach to my own life and work. It is a tool on which I have come to regularly rely, both personally and professionally, when working to bring about any major change. It is the basis for the powerful Make-It-Happen Model described in this book, which equally applies to individuals and organizations, and to both personal and professional aspirations.

Over the years, I've encountered Susan in many capacities—as a colleague, as a mentor, and as a friend. In each role, while able to be as tough as necessary to "get the job done," she has also proven herself to be among the wisest, most generous, and most bighearted people I have ever known.

This book continues that pattern. Susan doesn't hold back; she mines her years of experience for every insight and tip and word of advice that might make things a little easier for us than it was for her. And she doesn't sugarcoat it: she writes of the hard work ahead if we want to achieve our aspirations by taking on the lofty title of CEO of our own company (a.k.a., You, Inc.). She warns us that we can't do it alone and that we'll need to galvanize a team and our own personal board of directors. Between the lines, we sense that Susan herself wants to be the self-appointed first member of our team.

Knowing Susan for more than a decade as I have, I can assure you that sentiment is accurate. She has made it her mission to champion others to reach their dreams. And as your "virtual mentor," Susan's sage advice is always only an e-mail or a phone call away.

You'll find a lifetime of advice in the pages that follow. Savor these hard-earned lessons by one of America's leading businesswomen. Study them. Take them to heart. Then apply them to your own life's challenges and opportunities.

I can attest from firsthand experience that they're sound and that they can help you leapfrog toward your goals. If you work, they work.

When you hit any proverbial (and inevitable!) bumps in the road, you couldn't have a better colleague, mentor, and friend than Susan Bulkeley Butler to advise you how to move over, through, or around them.

You've already taken an invaluable first step by picking up this book, so I'm confident you're on the right track. I wish you great success as the CEO of You, Inc.!

Karen Page
Award-winning author and Founding Chair, Harvard Business School
Network of Women Alumnae
September 2005

A NOTE TO READERS

Andersen Consulting became Accenture in 2001. I joined the company when it was a part of Arthur Andersen & Co. For the sake of this book's brevity and clarity, I will call the company Accenture throughout.

Susan Bulkeley Butler, 2005

PART I

Laying the Groundwork

YOU ARE THE CEO OF YOU, INC.

"Become the change you want to see—those are words I live by."
—OPRAH WINFREY

f you are holding this book in your hands, you are in search of something, whether it's new strategies for improving your life or new techniques for advancing your career. Whatever your goal may be, the lessons I provide in these pages will give you the tools that will enable you to turn your dream into reality. How do I know? They are the same strategies that propelled me to be a top executive in the CEO suite of one of the world's largest companies.

Like any successful enterprise, your life needs a plan, a framework around which you can make smart decisions that will define your future.

Like any business that hopes to win, you need someone to oversee the big picture: someone who will identify the unique benefits you offer, as well as develop your package of skills and capabilities and the way you present them to the world. Who would be the best candidate for the job? Congratulations: I hereby promote you to CEO of You, Inc.—that is, CEO of your own life and career. Being the CEO of *any* entity is an important responsibility, but even more so now, as the entity's well-being starts and stops with *you*.

This is not a job you can "outsource" to someone else. Like any CEO position, there's a 110% commitment required to *make* things happen. The alternative? *Letting* things happen to You, Inc., such as falling prey to what others want you to be and not necessarily to what you want to become. Accepting this promotion to CEO brings significant responsibility. You, Inc.'s success or failure is in your hands.

The first order of business will be adopting a CEO mind-set. What does it mean to have a CEO mind-set? In essence, it means having a proactive orientation to getting whatever it is you want, and to taking a high-level perspective on all the different aspects of your life—career, finances, health, family and friends, personal growth—and achieving an optimal balance among them. This balance will change throughout your life, but as CEO of You, Inc., you will be in a position to continually make adjustments to achieve that equilibrium.

★ ★ ★

"Even if you're on the right track, you'll get run over if you just sit there."
—WILL ROGERS

Embracing Change

Because the world is always changing, your life is always changing, and the only thing you have any control over is how it changes. As the world shifts around you, it's your task to keep focused on where you want to go and to figure out, day in and day out, what you have to do to get there.

The process of change, which occurs at ever-faster levels of e-speed in our seemingly 24/7 workweeks, can be overwhelming. Do you think I'm overstating things, being too dramatic? Consider these facts: on an average day in the United States, approximately 11,000 babies are born, 6,000 people die, 7,000 marriages take place, and 3,000 divorces are finalized.

Important changes are taking place not only in your external environment but also *within* you. More than 2,400 years ago, Plato observed the following:

> *"As the years go by, time will change and even reverse many of your present opinions."*

Since yesterday, you yourself have changed. You're not only a day older, but what you aspire to in your life may have shifted in significant ways. Or, you may still desire the same things, but with even greater fervor and determination. Depending on your actions and their effectiveness, you're also a day closer to—or further from—your goals.

There is one overarching message to keep in mind as you read on: make things happen *for* you, don't just let them happen *to* you. This is the lesson that has played the biggest role in my own success story. The idea comprises two distinct disciplines: the first is learning to manage change, and the second is learning to be proactive. Why are these worth focusing on? A CEO's primary responsibility is to establish the vision and strategy for an organization—and the job of managing *strategy* is really a matter of managing *change*.

All of us must learn to deal with the inevitable tides of change, both external and internal, to create the results we want to see in our lives. We should not be threatened by the changes in our environment. Rather, we can learn to see more clearly the opportunities that lie just beyond these challenges.

Say, for example, you are hit hard with the news that your boss wants to transfer you to another city. How can you make this change work to your advantage? Can you lobby for a promotion if you do agree to move? A raise? Or, you may decide to leave the company so you don't have to pack up and move. Was it time to move on anyway? How can you now take those skills you learned and apply them to getting an even better position in a different company? Remember: each change—whether internal or external—provides you with a choice. *You* get to decide how it will play out in your life. Change can happen

Women Who Have Changed the World

If you simply take a look through history, you'll find countless examples of inspiring women from all walks of life who have literally helped to change the world—proving that women are some of the best change-masters I know. Here's a sampling:

- *Susan B. Anthony* (1820–1906) led the struggle to gain the vote for women. She devoted fifty years of her life to the suffrage movement and promoted social reform without ever having the right to vote. She said, "Cautious, careful people always casting about to preserve their reputation and social standing never can bring about reform. Those who are really in earnest, must be willing to be anything or nothing in the world's estimation." (She died fourteen years before the 19th amendment, which granted women the right to vote, was ratified in 1920.) In 1979, she became the first woman to be featured on a circulating U.S. coin.
- *Amelia Earhart* (1898–1937) was a pioneering woman in aviation who broke records and charted new territory. She once wrote, "Courage is the price that life expects for granting peace with yourself."
- *Golda Meir* (1898–1978) was the first woman foreign minister and prime minister of Israel, and one of the most visible women in international affairs from the 1950s until her death.
- *Mother Teresa* (1910–1997) was a Roman Catholic nun who won the Nobel Peace Prize in 1979 for her humanitarian work.
- *Babe Zaharias* (1911–1956) was the sports phenomenon of the 1930s and 1940s, astounding both sides of the Atlantic with her

to you—or *you* can *affect* change. It's a matter of assuming control, of taking initiative.

Affecting change made a key difference in my own career. Years ago, as I was working my way up the ladder at Accenture, I held a world headquarters position in its Chicago office. It was fine; I was happy, if

---

athletic performance. She openly challenged the leftover Victorian notions of what women could not and should not do athletically. Instrumental in establishing the women's professional golf tour, she set the stage for the rest of the century for the girls and women who followed her onto the greens. She demonstrated her wisdom when she said "You can't win them all—but you can try."

- *Indira Gandhi* (1917–1984) served as the first woman prime minister of India (from 1966–1977 and 1980–84). She said, "If I die today, every drop of my blood will invigorate the nation."
- *Margaret Thatcher* (1925–) not only served as the first woman prime minister of Great Britain but also, given her tenure from 1979 to 1990, was its longest continually serving prime minister in 150 years. Known as the "Iron Lady," she was both admired and despised. Although she reversed decades of decline and reinstated Great Britain as a major economic power, this brought about social friction.
- *Althea Gibson* (1927–2003) was the first African American to win at the U.S. Open and Wimbledon. She was also the first woman of color to compete at the U.S. Open in 1950.
- *Judith Rodin* (1944–) was named the president of the University of Pennsylvania, becoming the first woman to be named president of an Ivy League institution, and the first Penn alum to serve as its president. During her tenure, the reputation of the university grew dramatically. She currently serves as president of the Rockefeller Foundation, where she's been said to be a visionary leader who wants to reduce poverty around the world.

not incredibly challenged. But, I knew from my colleagues in New York there was more opportunity for career growth in their dynamic office. I also knew that my superior in Chicago would not support my transfer. I had many responsibilities that he would need to find someone else to take over if I left.

"All they can do is say no," I thought to myself as I got up the courage to ask for the transfer. And, at first, that is exactly what my superior said. I felt like my dreams had been crushed. But, I leveraged my relationships with my New York colleagues and, with their support, he finally conceded to let me go. I *made* it happen. And, it was at that point that my career really began to skyrocket!

Learning to manage change can apply to not only your career, but to any area of interest in your life. Being an investor in a Broadway show provided me with one of the best examples of what success in managing change is all about. Impressed with the score of a new musical written and directed by the creative team behind the Broadway hit *Les Misérables*, I was enticed into investing in *Jane Eyre*, a dramatized version of Charlotte Brontë's classic novel.

The musical earned standing ovations night after night from audience members who were bowled over by the entire cast's extraordinary performances. Indeed, the show earned five Tony Award nominations, including a "Best Actress" nomination for Marla Schaffel (who also won the Drama Desk and Outer Critics' Circle's "Best Actress" Awards) for her portrayal of Jane Eyre. However, the production closed on Broadway after a disappointingly short run of seven months.

How did the actors react to this unanticipated change in their lives? Did they curse the show's fate and vow to give up acting forever? Of course not. They didn't miss a beat. In fact, within a few short weeks, Marla was rehearsing lines for her starring role in a Gershwin musical at the Goodspeed Opera House.

These professional actors knew, as do all successful navigators of change, that no matter how negative a change may seem at the time, unintended benefits could result.

Without any conscious awareness of the Make-It-Happen Model put forth in the pages that follow, the actors instinctively followed their vision of being successful actors: envisioning the role, finding the right people to help, identifying the steps to get there, and navigating the unexpected ups and downs along the way.

Remember: change is a constant, but *your reaction to change is a choice.* You can let it overwhelm you, or you can proactively see change as an opportunity to bring about the most important experiences in your life. While it can be challenging, even fear inducing, it can also be exciting. Now that you are CEO of You, Inc., it is your responsibility to master the process of managing change.

Another way of making things happen *for* you, as opposed to letting them happen *to* you, is by being proactive. Take advantage of the everyday opportunities that come your way. Because change is a constant in our lives, sometimes the best things pop up when and where we least expect them. Even if you initially feel uncomfortable, being proactive and taking risks each day opens you up to opportunities that can make a difference. Consider some examples:

- At a party, someone mentions a position they're looking to fill for which you think you'd be perfect.
- While getting your nails done, you strike up a conversation with someone who happens to know someone with whom you would like to do business.
- You're on an airplane and notice that your seatmate works for an organization in which you're very interested.

As an example, I was once on a red-eye flight to Washington, D.C. and noticed the man sitting next to me had White House tags on his luggage. I've always had an avid interest in the goings-on of Capitol Hill, so I struck up a conversation with him. Amazingly, our talk led to an invitation to have breakfast at the White House mess while I was in town. As it turns out, this man's mission was to find women to fill many of the positions in the Reagan administration, which was looking to diversify its appointments.

He offered me an opportunity to consider an appointed position in the president's administration. I was incredibly flattered and considered leaving Accenture to pursue this exciting opportunity. However, a close advisor of mine helped me think through the decision. I was young and had not accomplished all I could achieve in the corporate world. There would always be time for other pursuits later. I felt he was right and declined the offer. But, as you can see, amazing things can begin with a friendly chat on a plane!

Be open to life's chance occurrences and unanticipated changes. See them for the opportunities that they are, and be proactive. Try to be receptive to whatever life puts in front of you because sometimes it can be better than anything you could have ever imagined.

★ ★ ★

In the chapters that follow, I will describe in detail the Make-It-Happen Model (MIH Model), which will help to guide you on your journey as CEO of You, Inc. By now you know that your level of success will depend on how well you manage change as well as by how proactive you are. But where do you start? How do you apply these ideas in your everyday life?

Success in making change happen involves a systematic approach consisting of four primary steps, each of which is dependent on the others. This model was developed through observing successful and unsuccessful strategies for navigating change. I even attribute my own career success to this process, and it served me well in helping my Accenture clients implement significant changes in their organizations (which ranged from *Fortune* 500 companies to the U.S. Navy).

I have used the MIH Model successfully, both in my personal and professional lives. For example, midway through my career, there was a major reorganization within my company. I decided that I needed to make sure that I was proactive in determining where I landed. I wanted to ensure that it was a place I wanted to be instead of a place where someone else wanted me to be. My vision and initiative—based on the Make-It-Happen Model—earned me a new position and a promotion to office managing partner of Accenture's Philadelphia office.

The secret of making things happen for You, Inc., is rooted in the MIH Model, which requires you to complete the following steps:

1. Set a clear *vision.*
2. Build a *team* that supports you.
3. Develop a detailed *plan.*
4. *Navigate* the journey.

The corporate world has had the benefit of leveraging these powerful principles to increase its revenues and profitability, as well as become more effective and efficient.

These lessons can also benefit You, Inc. The principles of managing change will help you, as the CEO of You, Inc., manage the tides of change and ultimately achieve anything that you envision.

Step 1: Envision Your Future (Determine Where You Want to Go)

Leaders have a vision for the future. As CEO, the leader of You, Inc., you should have a vision for your career and life—just as a corporate CEO has a vision for her company's future—for the next twenty-four hours, week, month, year, five years, or lifetime. The goal is to make the results you want to see happen, *happen.*

It's important that your vision creates a compelling picture, not only to motivate others, but also to spur yourself on. As the CEO of You, Inc., it is absolutely essential for you to make things happen *for* you, rather than let them happen *to* you. Creating a solid strategy is the first step in ensuring this key piece is in place.

Think about it: over the next two to three years, what would you like to be able to say you have achieved? A good example might be "Within the next two years, I intend to be promoted within my company," or "I will stick to a regular exercise routine for the foreseeable future that will help ensure my health and well-being as a CEO" or perhaps "I will return to the workforce and join an organization that will provide me with promotion opportunities as well as the lifestyle that I need to raise my children."

Step 2: Recruit a Team to Support Your Vision

How are you going to make your vision a reality? One human being can accomplish a great deal, but most great visions require the cooperation of many people working collaboratively. Your team is all about marshaling and empowering the necessary human resources to help you realize your vision.

To achieve success as CEO of You, Inc., you will need people on your team to help make it happen. If you think about where you are today and how you got here, you'll realize that there have always been people (such as friends, role models, mentors, teachers) who have helped you make things happen; you didn't do it all by yourself.

Your team will serve as the board of directors for You, Inc., and will be available to provide advice and counsel regarding your goals and how to achieve them. You should be able to depend on them to ask you tough questions, the kind you need to best focus your efforts. They will become your sounding board and will have ideas and alternatives that you may have not even considered. By helping you think through various paths to success, your options will become clearer, more realistic, and less daunting.

Step 3: Develop Your Plan (Determine What You Need to Do and How to Do It)

Achieving your vision means considering the details of what is required to bring your aspiration to life. What kinds of skills, experiences, and knowledge will it entail? To begin to develop the plan for You, Inc., ask, "Who am I today, and who do I need to become to accomplish my goals? What are the steps I need to take to move from today to tomorrow?"

Ensure the achievement of your vision by developing a plan to get you from where you are to where you want to be. As an image, I like to think of the TripTik provided by AAA when I drove from Tucson,

Arizona, to Florence, Oregon. The TripTik showed the routes to follow, the places to eat, the rest stops, the miles between major cities, and the total hours it would take to make the drive. Your plan is like a Trip-Tik, a detailed map with milestones to keep you on track.

Step 4: Navigate Your Journey (and Overcome Obstacles along the Way)

Once you have your vision, team, and plan in place, it's time to take action and begin running You, Inc. on a day-to-day basis. This will involve the practicalities—from conducting a good meeting to effectively managing your finances. It will also mean taking a good, hard look at yourself through the eyes of your "customers," whether that means your superiors, your clients, or the people interviewing you for a position. How are you presenting You, Inc. to the world? Are you marketing yourself as effectively as you would like?

While enacting the plan for You, Inc., monitor what is going on around you, and take advantage of your environment. Note the effectiveness of all your actions. And, as you encounter unanticipated events, figure out how to adjust your plan and its implementation accordingly. You can modify your strategy to minimize the threat posed by new risks, or even expand it to take advantage of new opportunities. This is what keeps you on course. You have a destination, a crew, and a map—but you still need to be awake, alert, and not on autopilot to make sure you get to where you want to go.

This is a great opportunity to see if you're heading in the right direction and to readjust your efforts when necessary. Even the best-made plans should be changed when they aren't as effective as anticipated.

★ ★ ★

The Make-It-Happen Model is a tool to help keep you on track as you grow as CEO of You, Inc., and it will help you avoid many common stumbling blocks. For example, people often make the mistake of short-term, or small-picture, thinking. They jump into planning without sufficiently thinking their vision through. Or, they get stuck working their way down their "to do" lists without taking the time to get their team on board.

As you become accustomed to your new position, the mind-set of a CEO will become a way of being.

The following chapter will show you what every CEO knows: a winning strategy is essential if you plan to win. While you develop your strategy, which will in turn define your vision for You, Inc., you will continually see opportunities to take the initiative and manage change to your advantage. This is the backbone of the Make-It-Happen Model and is integral to achieving your goal(s).

★ ★ ★

"Write what should not be forgotten."
—ISABELLE ALLENDE

Additionally, this is a good time to begin to record your thoughts as you embark upon your journey as CEO of You, Inc. I have often wished I had written my thoughts and goals in a journal over the past forty years so I could see how they have shifted over time. I would be fascinated to look back and be able to exactly recount my dreams . . . and see how successful I was at making them happen.

To help you get started with your journal, I have included thoughts and advice on journaling from a few friends. It is a personal endeavor, of course, but their words may inspire you to get started right away. As you read on, you'll note that I've included thoughts for reflection at the end of each chapter. They are designed to inspire you to be self-aware as you navigate your journey. As you read and process them, use your journal to record your thoughts and feelings.

A Roundup of Thoughts on Keeping a Journal

From **Carla Paonessa**, President, CJAssociates:

- *Begin.* Journaling started for me as a yearly affair. I retreated annually for a week to a health spa in Mexico. It was my way to decompress from a frantic, full "workyear." On Friday afternoons, I would swing under a big oak tree, gazing at Mt. Kuchima, dreaming and writing about what my life would be like the next year. I did that for twenty-three years but discovered after retirement that I could now do that every day — and what pleasure it has been.

- *Find the Right Spot.* I have to find the right spot to write. In Scottsdale, Arizona it is on my back porch, gazing at the desert, the mountains, and the golf course that begs me to lower my score next time. In Chicago, it's on my front porch gazing at Lake Michigan, Lincoln Park, and the city. In other spaces, I just need to be outside. Wherever you choose, go back there again and again. It becomes sacred space. Journalist, novelist, and screenwriter Dan Wakefield, in his book, *Creating from the Spirit: Living Each Day as a Creative Act*, says, "I've always had a sense of the places where I could write and where I couldn't write." I agree.

- *Find the Right Time.* I write early in the morning, with a cup of coffee, right after I've had some private time to read. That's when I'm freshest. That's when I'm least committed to other activities. That's when I'm most reflective. On occasion it happens in the early evening, before the dinner hour. At that hour, however, I'm compelled to write because something has just happened or I've had something on my mind all day that I just couldn't get to until the sun began to set. Morning tide works better for me than evening tide.

continued on next page

- *Find the Subject.* There's not a "right" subject. Whatever comes to mind is OK. Sometimes it's about nature; sometimes it's about how I feel; other times it's about something troubling me or giving me joy. Once I jotted down memories I had from childhood to present day, filling three pages, typewritten, single-spaced, double-columned. That was inspired by reading Jack Macguire's *The Power of Personal Storytelling: Spinning Tales to Connect with Others.* I wondered if my three pages were too many or too few. Another time, I recorded a list of turning points in my life. Each of those became a separate subject for an entry. The "what" doesn't matter. The "why" does.

- *Find the Right Why.* Why journal, and for whom? Journaling is for you. If you journal with the hope that someone else would probably want to read it, you may find you are disappointed. I just read *The Unabridged Journals of Sylvia Plath: 1950–1962*, edited by Karen V. Kukil. Whew! Plath, a notable American poet, author, and Fulbright Scholar in Cambridge, England, started journaling at the age of eleven and continued until her death at thirty, but those adult journals covering the twelve years from 1950 to 1962 had more detail than I asked for. I should have read the abridged version (no offense intended). She probably didn't write those journals with the hope that they would someday be read by others.

Your journal is not a stage. It shouldn't be written for an audience. It's for you. Be honest. Write as though you won't know who you really are unless you write. Write for yourself. The act of writing is soul food. And if someone else happens to read it someday, so be it.

From **Julie Hendon** and friends, Purdue University:
Journaling is all about capturing how you feel. Some pointers:

- Take your journal (or something on which you can record thoughts) wherever you go.
- Write everything that you feel—the good and the bad.
- Write raw, nondiscretionary thought, just as you would think or talk to yourself.
- If you miss a day, it's OK. Don't feel like you have to play catch up.
- Keep the journal private and well hidden, so you never hold back anything.
- Use journals as "learning experiences" in your life. Look back at where you've been and how far you've come.

From **Eric Young**, Accenture:
For some, journaling comes naturally as a relaxing, constructive activity. For others, it can be a dreaded chore. I encourage people to try journaling if they haven't before as a way to get ideas and concepts out of their overloaded brains and onto paper (or at least into their laptops' memories).

Journaling for me is having a written conversation with myself about most any topic: perhaps something in the news, a controversial issue for which I don't have an easy answer, an unexpected observation I have made during the day, or concerns that are worrying me. Why is this on my mind? Why did I notice that? Why am I moved by this? What do I think about that? What might I do in response? What does this say about me, my beliefs, my priorities, my values, and my character?

Writing things out allows me to translate feelings and ambiguities into something concrete, if only words that don't necessarily solve or resolve the issue. In the process, I often uncover insights or solutions, or just have the freedom to formulate ideas and opinions. Perhaps most interesting is picking up a journal from five years ago to read how my thinking and attitudes have changed (hopefully for the better).

CHAPTER 1 RECAP

LESSON #1: Become CEO of You, Inc., with a CEO mind-set.

LESSON #2: Change happens, but your reaction is your choice.

LESSON #3: Make things happen *for* you, don't let them happen *to* you.

ACTION ITEMS:

- Read about what is happening in the world. Read business magazines to learn from business leaders, industry publications to learn the business issues in your industry, or newspapers to learn about happenings around the world. Make notes about what is happening in the world, the issues, characteristics of great leaders, and so forth.

- Read about leaders and learn from them. For example, Joe Forehand, chairman of Accenture, read about Jack Welch and his leadership style; Rudy Giuliani, mayor of New York City during 9/11, read about Winston Churchill and how he led his country through World War II.

REFLECT AND RECORD:

- How do you normally react to change? Do you avoid it at all costs? Do you embrace it as an exciting challenge? Why do you react one way or another?

- What are your feelings about being a CEO, concerns, things you want to "make" happen for you, and the major steps and the time frame necessary to make them happen?

- Recall the last time you were socially proactive. What came of it? A new contact? A lead on a job? Helpful advice? Did you learn something new? How did you obtain these outcomes from this social activity?

- Think of an upcoming opportunity to affect change. Are you up for an evaluation, a job interview, or a promotion? How can you be proactive in *making* the desired result happen?

CREATE THE VISION FOR YOU, INC.

"Vision is the art of seeing things invisible."
—JONATHAN SWIFT

The first step toward creating a vision for You, Inc. is developing a strategy that helps you crystallize what you really *want* to do, can do, and *must* do to achieve your vision.

When I was a young girl, my goal was to sell more Girl Scout cookies than anyone else in my troop. Without even knowing what the word *strategy* meant, I intuitively took the time to come up with one.

For example, instead of running outside to start knocking on every door I saw, I thought about to whom I might sell (and that the largest families without Girl Scouts might buy the most cookies from me), where to sell (and which high traffic locations might yield the most sales to passersby), and how and when I might make more time to put into selling cookies (and I put off doing my homework until after dinner so I could sell cookies after school). My strategy paid off; I did end up selling the most cookies.

Setting up a concrete strategy to achieve your vision is essential. Igor Ansoff, the author of the 1965 book *Corporate Strategy*, is considered the godfather of corporate strategy. He is credited with creating the vocabulary and systems that address strategic questions such as which strengths to make use of, how to achieve growth, and how to manage the process. His model of strategic planning includes three points:

1. Observing where you are (which strengths to make use of)
2. Identifying where you want to be (how to achieve growth)
3. Determining the actions that will take you there (how to manage the process)

How do you chart your course? Here are some exercises that can help put things in perspective. Remember, the ultimate goal is to have a baseline that outlines your vision. This helps you evaluate how you are doing with regard to making progress toward achieving your vision, or to alter your goal or path based on what you learn as you move forward.

1. Where Are You Now?

Develop an honest assessment of your current capabilities, your distinguishing strengths, and the areas for improvement. What are your skills and capabilities? What have you accomplished? Who are your advocates? How have you been evaluated? What are the perceptions others have of you? What are the areas in which you need to improve? What patterns do you see in yourself—those you like and those you may not like? What are your real strengths? How is your confidence? What do you do to have fun, and what joy do you get out of your work?

2. Where Do You Want to Be?

Dream. What would you like to accomplish? In what time frame? What capabilities do you need to have? What do you need to accomplish and achieve? Your specific objectives and goals will lead you to develop an appropriate strategy and to find the resources necessary to execute it (for example, mentors, connections, and time), all of which will be discussed in chapters that follow.

3. What Actions Will Take You to Where You Want to Be?

How will you develop skills and capabilities? What responsibilities do you need to have and how and when will you get them? How do you meet people to help you achieve your goals?

Your strategy should be defined in a way that you can describe it in thirty seconds, or the period of a proverbial elevator ride. (That's why it's called an elevator speech.) For example, my strategy for Susan Butler, Inc. is to impact zillions of women and girls and to be recognized as an authority on mentoring and the development of women leaders.

★ ★ ★

"Nothing happens unless first a dream."
—CARL SANDBURG

The Secret of Visioning

The time I've invested over the years in thinking about what I wanted most in my life has given me some of the greatest return.

It's rare that sheer luck will lead you to the life that you envision. The stories of quirks of fate that lead certain people to being "discovered" are more legend than fact. Typically, those who make it to the top do so with a combination of clear goals, a plan to reach them, and hard work (with a little bit of luck thrown in).

With a specific vision in place, you can prepare yourself to be in the right place at the right time. It takes planning and effort to be in a position where you are the next in line for the promotion or the best candidate for the job opening. Your vision can help you get there.

What happens when you don't take the time to fully plan things in advance either is (1) nothing or (2) something that is less than what it could have been. Successful companies, as well as successful people, never rest on their laurels. They are always aspiring to be more, to do more, and to excel.

A top executive at Intel recently told me there are three things she blocks out time for each day: lunch, exercise, and thinking time. The latter is when she takes a quiet moment to think about whether she's on the right track to reach her goal, whether that be getting the report done by six o'clock or getting the promotion by year's end. Just like the most successful executives, you need to commit to investing the necessary time thinking and even writing out your vision for your future.

Think about it—each of us has the same 8,760 hours to live every year. Isn't it worth spending *at least* 1% of your time deciding what you want most and planning how to use that time? That's just 88 hours a year, or less than two hours a week. Pick a Friday afternoon or a weekend morning to give yourself the luxury of "thinking time" to evaluate where you are and where you are going, rather than leave things to chance—or to someone else's will!

Learning about Strategy from the Girl Scouts

One of the best places I learned about setting strategy and achieving goals was while serving on the national board of directors of the Girl Scouts of the USA (GSUSA). The organization's legendary leader at the time, Frances Hesselbein, had risen from a local volunteer Girl Scout troop leader to the CEO of the national organization. Her success in bringing the Girl Scouts back from near demise between 1976 and 1990 was documented in a Harvard Business School case study—and recognized with a Presidential Medal of Freedom, America's highest civilian honor. Frances is one of the most organized people I have ever met, but her real secret weapons were always thinking of the individual Girl Scout and putting the girl's interests at the heart of every decision she made. Frances was convinced that doing so on every occasion was the best way of enhancing the Girl Scout "brand," and would allow the organization to accomplish its strategic objective of interesting even more girls in joining.

Over the years, the mission statement of Girl Scouts of the USA has evolved from:

"To help girls grow and reach their own great potential,"

to

"To inspire girls with the highest ideals of character, conduct, patriotism, and service that they may become happy resourceful citizens."

Frances Hesselbein explains, "We don't strive for superior or excellent management. We strive to manage for the mission: We never lose sight of the fact that we are in this business to help girls grow. Having such a strong mission increases our managerial productivity—people 'buy into' what we do and thus motivation increases. We work very hard, all of us, to remember why we are working."

One strategy GSUSA used to meet this mission was to provide opportunities for every girl to participate in a wide variety of experiences. These activities ranged from career exploration, recreation, leadership, current events, sports, planning, business, fashion, environmental protection, and community service to exploring cultural heritage and celebrating being a girl.

Having Trouble Envisioning What You Want?

You may not have realized it, but you're on a train. Your current life path, your current position, and your current place of work represent tracks that are moving you along in your life. Do you like where you're heading?

If you don't care where you're going, any train will do. If you do care, however, it's important to make sure you're on the right one. Don't just let yourself go for a ride—make sure you're going someplace you want to be.

There may be times in your life when you're not positive about what you want. For example, you may feel pulled in many different directions. Alternately, you may be going through a period when nothing seems to ignite your deepest passions. This is a sign that it's time to live by my motto: "Make things happen *for* you." Even if nothing excites you at the moment, you still need to make proactive decisions about where you are going. You can change course along the way, but wouldn't you rather be actively in control of the vision for your life than just floating along with the current?

Let's start with some questions to help stimulate your thinking:

- If your "dream job" came through for you, how would you describe it? Would it be as an executive of a global corporation or working in your own cozy office at home? Would you be managing a team of bright corporate stars or running your own small business? Why would you want one versus the other?

- If you were given an extra twenty-four hours every week, how would you want to spend that time? If you could spend a week on yourself—free of all obligations and free of guilt—what would you choose to do during that week and why?

- Who do you most envy, and why? Is there someone who currently has the dream job you're looking for? Describe them, in terms of their capabilities and responsibilities. If you were in their position, or a similar one, what would you like to accomplish a few years down the line?

◆ Sometimes when you're really stuck, it helps to think of some of the things you know you *don't* want. Look at the jobs you wouldn't take, even if they paid twice what you're making now. What do they have in common? What's the opposite characteristic? Does that suggest any new ideas to you about what you *do* want in a job?

◆ Now, ask yourself, "If I could design my life just the way I want it, how would I do it?" Describe the elements of your ideal scenario—the people, places, things and experiences that would all be a part of it. It's important to describe these in such a way that it will both create a clear picture in your mind and allow you to describe it clearly to others.

◆ Keeping in mind what you hope to achieve in three to five years, write yourself a letter and date it three to five years from now. Envision what your life will look like, and write a detailed description of it.

Sample: *Dear Susan, In the past three years, my institute has assisted six* Fortune *500 companies in developing women leaders, and we annually conduct two large (200–300 person) Leadership Seminars. In addition, my book,* Become the CEO of You, Inc., *is very successful, and I'm working on a second book as a follow-up.*

◆ Bringing the goals you set for yourself in this letter one step closer into the present, write yourself another letter and date it one year from now. Envision what your life will be like then, and write a detailed enough description of it to be able to provide a clear picture to the team you will assemble to help you achieve it.

Sample: *Dear Susan, In the last year, my book has been published and has received rave reviews from my readers. I have participated in six conferences, been a keynote speaker at eight events, and designed a five day sabbatical for women. Oh, and my company is profitable!*

◆ How will you know if you have achieved your vision? How will you measure your accomplishments?

Sample: *Within one year, my institute will have a positive cash flow, and I will have sold 2,500 copies of my book.*

Your answers should give you a good start in developing your goals. For example, what themes do you see running through your responses? Are you attracted to positions that allow you to expand your knowledge? Manage resources? Lead a team? Write down a list of career options that would allow you to pursue your interests. You can be as broad as you like at first, and then tailor it down as you think more about your interests and capabilities. Be specific enough so that you can focus on the steps necessary to move You, Inc. forward.

Don't wait for someone to tap you on the shoulder to give you a vision for your future! You need to be in charge of the process. And be sure to base your vision on today's reality, not on something you hope will happen in the future.

Once you have a sense of your aspiration, the next step is to convince yourself that you can actually make it happen. To do this, make sure a few things are true:

- The tasks that need to be accomplished and the time frame allowed are within reason.
- You are willing to take the risk to do whatever it takes to make it happen.
- You are willing to pay the price to do whatever it takes to make it happen.

With these elements in place, you are ready to make your vision a reality—well, almost. You must also take finding balance into account. Striving to live a balanced life is an important goal in itself. Your daily existence is more than "becoming president of my company" or "starting my own catering business" or even "balancing career and motherhood."

When you make your plan, be sure to think through all aspects of having a balanced life:

- Career
- Family and friends
- Health and well-being
- Environment (home, office, community)

- Financial security
- Enjoyment of life (having fun)

What is the importance of balance? Think of each category of life as a spoke on a wheel. The wheel will squeak if one of the categories is off kilter. Most commonly, people put a disproportionate emphasis on their careers, leaving family and health to suffer. This eventually becomes unproductive. What happens when people's careers take over their lives without time for proper rest and recovery? Burnout.

It's also important to accept that some goals are incompatible, that not everything is of equal importance to you, and that choosing is necessary. You may not be able to become the first woman senior vice president (SVP) at a *Fortune* 500 corporation *and* raise and homeschool your children. (Who is?) You may not be able to become a top investment banker *and* a competitive sailor. However, you could become a *Fortune* 500 SVP and still spend evenings and most weekends with your kids. Or you could become a successful banker and take sailing vacations. Balance does not necessarily mean doing without.

★ ★ ★

When I started my career, I did not have a comprehensive master vision. I didn't know then what I know now. But, I did make a series of two-to-four-year plans that kept me on track.

My initial plan on day one was simply to make an annual salary of $10,000—nearly double my starting salary—which was probably the amount my father made. Once I achieved that goal, I focused on the major milestone of promotion to manager. Soon after that, my mentors convinced me that my next goal should be making partner. And from then on, as opportunities arose, I continued to develop my leadership expertise as a partner, ultimately from the Office of the CEO.

In this age of rapid change, your vision for You, Inc. is likely to be a moving target as you take into account an ever shifting environment. That is why determining your strategy is not so much a matter of coming up with a set-in-stone plan as it is having a strategic focus for your efforts. At the same time, you want to also seek to capitalize on new opportunities that are created by change.

A good example of this is the United Parcel Service (UPS). Years ago, UPS was simply a delivery service that was quicker than the U.S. Postal Service. With its trademark brown trucks and brown uniformed employees, it was a trusted delivery option. Then, along came FedEx. This fierce competitor forced UPS to make some strategic changes to retain market share. Now, it has extended more value to its customers by consolidating with Mail Boxes Etc. to provide shipping materials as well as post office services, copying, and faxing. This added value has enabled UPS to remain an industry leader. But FedEx has now made a similar acquisition with Kinko's. What's next?

Likewise, you must examine the ways and the arenas in which you can add value and be on the constant lookout for new opportunities. Continually revisit your vision. Remember that if there is a new opportunity or other information, your vision can be changed to take a new direction. After all, the environment changes almost daily. The needs of your "customer" (whether your employer or your clients) change. You yourself are likely to change. Make sure your vision is still on target!

CHAPTER 2 RECAP

LESSON #4: Develop the vision for You, Inc.

LESSON #5: Allocate thinking time for You, Inc.

LESSON #6: Base your vision on today's reality, not on what you hope will happen.

ACTION ITEMS:

◆ Draft your vision and high level plan for You, Inc. Set your sights high, and remember you should be able to describe it in a thirty-second "elevator speech."

◆ Schedule time (thinking time) to review your vision and progress, and to update it if things have changed.

REFLECT AND RECORD:

- Look to your past experiences to learn how you usually define the goals you want to achieve. Is there a pattern? Does it provide results? Are you where you want to be?
- Where are you currently, and what have you achieved in the past year or two? What have you not achieved?
- What are the two or three primary tasks you need to complete to achieve your vision?
- What do you want to have accomplished in the next three to five years? This is a new twist on the question: where do you want to be in five years? Focusing on what you want to accomplish guides you to the tangible things you can do, not just abstract hope.
- How will you define a balanced life based on the "spokes of your wheel?" How will this affect your vision for You, Inc.?

-3-

BUILD YOUR TEAM

"No one is wise enough by himself."

—PLAUTUS

The second step in the Make-It-Happen Model is to marshal the necessary people to realize your vision. One of the most important lessons you'll learn is that you can accomplish very few great things alone. Business—and life—is a team sport, and getting other people on board to help you reach your goal is critical. In fact, it's especially crucial to involve people from the start who can "see further" than you're able to, so that you can benefit from their experience and counsel.

The crucial question is *which* people. Will their influence on you be positive, negative, or neutral? You need to have as much control over this as possible, which is why it's so important to proactively select and build your team. While the specific people on your team will change over the course of time, you will always need people to fill the roles of expert, mentor, coach, and other teammates.

Your Board of Directors

Now that you are the CEO, you'll want to make sure that You, Inc. is supported by a "board of directors." Although these people will not have formal meetings together, they will provide you with trusted advice and counsel about your strategy and ultimately will help you to achieve your vision. Choosing the right people for your board of directors is crucial. They will provide you with (1) input on your strategy and (2) advice and counsel as you begin to implement your plan to achieve the goals of your strategy. Some of my best learning experiences have come from my team of advisors, and I'm confident that they will be a significant source of learning to you.

Here is a summary of the benefits of having a board of directors:

- You'll have trusted supporters who will listen to you and provide you with honest feedback.
- Your team will open doors for you and will act as mentors, advocates, and role models to help you get your promotion or land your next career opportunity.

Recruiting Your Team

Once you have decided on the types of people to have on your team, you need to think about which specific individuals in those categories would likely be able and willing to help. The criteria to consider include not only a person's industry and functional expertise, but also whether that person is "people-focused"—that is, interested in helping others, including women, achieve. The latter quality is found in people who are not only well respected in their field but who also make it a point to help others get promoted, to listen, and to give of their time.

Although your team will grow gradually, you should be proactive about seeking out those who fit your criteria and who have a wide strategic network. As certain relationships develop, you will be able to sense who is willing to come on board. An ideal member of your team will be willing and able to meet with you, either formally or informally, open doors for you, and be an advocate for you when appropriate.

Keep in mind that most people enjoy helping others achieve success. Not only will the philanthropy make them feel good about themselves, they will likely be flattered by your interest in their expertise. They may have even gone through your same experience and can share lessons learned.

Women especially have a tendency not to reach out for help. Whether it's the fear of seeming incompetent or the tacit admission that you don't know 100% of everything, it is crucial that you know when to ask for help from your team. And, at the risk of stating the obvious, learn from the advice they give you. If you go back a second and third time with the same question, they may become unsure about your ability to handle the task.

Many people start out with an informal board, such as the family members and friends they naturally trust and turn to for advice and counsel on such matters as revising their resume or considering a career change. However, as you advance in your career, you will find you'll need expert advice from more objective sources.

I encourage you to develop an outstanding team of advisors, bringing together the best minds you know from a wide range of disciplines. Your board of directors can include colleagues, former bosses or teachers, industry leaders, family, and even those friends of yours who tend to look at life in a different way.

The primary categories of people you'll want to consider for your team include experts, mentors, and your personal services team that will keep your life running smoothly. It will be helpful to have both genders and different cultures represented, depending on your goal.

Your aspiration will drive your team requirements. For example, if you are starting your own company, seek out someone who has experience with startups. If you are appointed to head an organization that reports to a board of directors, include someone on your team who has reported to a board of directors. When I was at Accenture, my team included both peers and people in more senior positions. Now, I look for people who help or want to help women achieve all they want to achieve.

- ◆ *Experts*

  There are two primary ways of learning: first, through the tedious and time-consuming process of trial and error, and second, by absorbing the experience of others. Obviously, you can shorten your learning curve by pursuing the second route. Go to where the knowledge and experience is. I've learned a great deal throughout my life and career by observing people, and even organizations, that were successful, and then analyzing what made them so. Your direct supervisors and others with whom you work would be included in these categories.

  Looking at it from a corporate model, Accenture's clients turn to the company for a trusted team of experts to help them make difficult decisions or solve challenging problems. Seeking this kind of help is not an admission of weakness. Remember, "It takes diamonds to cut diamonds."

- ◆ *Mentors*

  The term *mentor* comes from Homer's *Odyssey*. According to Homer, while Odysseus was away, the education of his son Telemachus was entrusted to a man named Mentor. Both the broad definition of *mentor* (a trusted counselor or guide) and the word's more specific sense (a tutor or coach) honor Odysseus's friend.

  Mentors serve as trusted advisors and personal coaches, and can help by opening doors and making opportunities happen for you. These are people who you respect and trust, who have confidence in you, and, most important, whose input you value. Although mentors can be of either gender, I would suggest that you enlist the help of people of both genders and of diverse backgrounds who can provide you with valuable breadth of perspective.

One mentee of mine wisely noted that it's important not to assume your mentor should necessarily be like you. Although it may seem sensible that women and other minorities seek out mentors who share similar experiences, you risk closing doors to those who may have a different perspective. Always keep an open mind.

◆ *Personal Services Team*
Your personal services team consists of those professionals, such as your accountant or lawyer, to whom you delegate certain critical tasks. These are people with whom you entrust your important personal and professional needs. Unless you happen to be a trained accountant, is it really worth your time to do your own taxes? Your time is valuable, and by including these professionals on your team, you recognize what every smart CEO knows: delegate, delegate, delegate.

What Happens When You Don't Have the Right People on Your Team?

Sometimes, when I ask people whether they have mentors to help them achieve their goals, they admit they don't. To me, it is no surprise that such people are not able to achieve their goals. In other cases, they have attached their career to people (perhaps even their supervisors or managers) who are unable or unwilling to help them achieve their goals, either because these people are not on the right career track to be great help, or because they themselves are not high achievers or developers of women.

What happens when your team doesn't have the right people on it? You might make the biggest mistake of your career. You might make the wrong assumptions, or talk to the wrong people. You might not find out what you don't know.

I once came close to losing a career-making promotion. A number of years ago, I was asked to be the managing partner of the Office of the CEO at Accenture. I consulted numerous people to help me think through my decision. However, I did not include anyone who was actually working directly with the CEO, the people with whom I would be working. As a result, I made some inaccurate assumptions about what the job entailed. Because I had feared that it was a glorified administrative job, my initial response to the offer was no!

A friend of mine, and also of the CEO, called me to let me know that I had made a mistake. He described what the job actually would entail. He convinced me that it was the absolute right next opportunity for me, one that would provide me with many skills that would serve me in retirement when I might choose to serve on a board of directors. In retrospect, I am very thankful for this good counsel, as what he said turned out to be exactly right. If he hadn't jumped on board my team at the last minute, I would have missed my opportunity to be front and center in creating the future of our organization, which eventually became Accenture.

How to Use Your Team

Time is precious. No one has enough time to do everything they want to do for themselves, let alone for others. However, I have found that most people are willing to help you if you are respectful and use their time in a focused and efficient manner. Plan the time required; let them know the subject of the conversation; and be sure you use their time wisely. Following your conversations, be sure to thank them and provide them with feedback on the results of your discussion, especially if they provided you with a specific recommendation or contact on which you took action. This shows respect for their advice and demonstrates your responsiveness.

Your interaction may be as simple as an e-mail, a telephone conversation, or a meeting over a cup of coffee. It might be an informal conversation after a meeting to ask, "Would you give me feedback on my presentation?" or even a formal review. Don't forget to ask for specific examples. And, in every case, the more timely the feedback, the better. It's best to solicit comments while a particular situation is still fresh in someone's mind.

When to Change Your Team

Your team will change depending on your needs. Over the years, my team members have come and gone as they helped me choose a focus in college and advised me on resume writing, asking for a raise, and dealing with difficult coworkers. Now that I've created the Susan Bulkeley Butler Institute for the Development of Women Leaders, I am looking for advice on how to cast my net into new areas in which I can influence as many women as possible. The people I now have on my team include other women leaders who are policy makers and who lead national organizations, and CEOs who want to develop women leaders in their organizations. The team you build just depends on where you are in your life at a particular moment and where you want to go.

Some people on your team will remain there over the years, while you add new ones who can be of help as you develop new goals. For example, the goal of one of my mentees was to become a senior executive in her organization. We talked about her time frame, the experiences she still needed to have, and the people on her team who were going to help make it happen. After our conversation, I put her in touch with two people I felt could be helpful to her in achieving her goals. Her team changed as a result of our telephone call.

Another mentee was planning a women's leadership development conference in Ohio. Through our mentoring conversations, we identified the steps she needed to take to build her confidence and to make the conference a success. She certainly had the passion for the conference, and the talent to make it happen. But she hadn't done anything this grand and needed a coach to support her. The conference ended up being a huge success.

Always keep your eye out for new opportunities and for new team members who can help you meet your goals.

The Most Valuable Players on Your Team: Mentors

As you can see, mentors not only are a part of your team, they are the individuals who help you build your team. Mentors are not the luxury of a lucky few—they are absolutely essential to everyone, no matter what you are doing. Unlike others on your team, who will help you reach specific goals, mentors are those you can truly count on for much needed encouragement as well as explicit advice. With a mentor on your side, your vision will become reachable.

I've discussed work issues with women and men at various stages of their lives. Whenever any of them have expressed displeasure with how their careers are going, I have asked whether or not they have a mentor. Invariably, they don't.

What should you look for in a mentor? You'll want him or her to be someone whose input you value, someone you respect and trust, someone who has confidence in you, and someone who has something you need—whether knowledge, resources, or judgment. You will have many mentors throughout your life and career. They change over time because the needs they serve are specific to a particular point in time. In college, you may have professors as mentors. At work, they'll likely be senior colleagues. Others may include friends or members of your family.

The process of finding a mentor will be different for everyone. The key is knowing where you want to go and always looking out for those who can help you get there. Once you make a habit of this, it will become second nature.

So, what exactly does a mentor do? A mentor is an advisor or a role model, someone with whom you can talk about where you want to go and how you should go about getting there. You can discuss with your mentor the approach you are taking, questions you have, and problems that you have encountered. A mentor is someone whose advice you value, who champions you, who will be an advocate for you, and who believes in you and your abilities.

There are some ideal mentor characteristics:

- Mentors have a responsibility to be honest with you, the mentee. They should be candid about your relative strengths and weaknesses. A mentor should discuss with you how you can improve, whether your vision is attainable, and, if so, what the best approach is to make it a reality.

- A successful mentor is a good listener, not just a problem solver giving advice. As a mentee, sometimes all you need is someone to talk to and not necessarily to solve your problems. I have found that just by talking to someone who is a good listener, I can usually come up with the right answer myself.
- A mentor should encourage you to do things of which they think you're capable—even if you're not yet sure you can.

However, finding a mentor who is willing to help you achieve your goals is not enough. You, as a mentee, must manage the relationship according to certain guidelines. A mentee needs to take responsibility for her own decisions, while accepting input from her mentor. A mentor can even state emphatically, "This is what you should do;" however, a mentee must weigh the pros and cons of the mentor's input. (The flip side is that if a mentee doesn't take her mentor's advice, her mentor may not want to continue in the relationship.)

Here are some guidelines for becoming the ideal mentee:

- Mentees should ask questions to make sure they absolutely understand their mentor's input.
- A successful mentoring relationship requires trust and confidence. Don't ever break the trust between you and a mentor. Participants in a true relationship respect the boundaries of trust. However, if you feel that the information you receive from your mentor may not be correct or appropriate, I would find a way to discuss your concern with another trusted advisor. In many cases, I found that following my "gut" usually has led me in the right direction.
- As a mentee, you should always ask for feedback (for example, "How did I do?"). Timely feedback is essential to improving your skills and capabilities.

I definitely wouldn't be where I am today without my mentors. A mentor will help to point you in the right direction and to make sure you focus on the right things.

Mentor Case Studies

Eric Young, Accenture:

I have a mentor who I feel captures the great value that mentors ideally offer to a mentee. Mentors are not parents; because you may not want to disappoint or disclose intimacies to your parents, building a bond of trust with them is not easily achieved. Effective mentors can get in deep with mentees to discuss family matters and political issues, personal addictions or harmful behaviors, drinking and drug abuse, etc. I feel completely free and open talking with my mentor about anything. We now meet up once or twice per year and cover all the basic topics of life: work, finances, relationships, family, health, faith. He is loving, gentle, encouraging, wise, humorous, and honest. I leave my time with him feeling overwhelmingly loved, accepted, and understood. He plays a beautiful role, a combination of parent, priest, counselor, coach, mentor, friend, and boss.

Rick Smith, Right Management Consultants:

A number of years ago, I had the opportunity to work closely with my mentor on a large project. I had periodically sought out this person to ask for advice and get ideas. He was a senior leader who I really admired and who seemed to have good insight. In preparation for one of the large project meetings, I was asked to join in performing in a fun skit and — of all things — impersonate my mentor.

At first I was flattered and looked forward to having a little fun at this prospect! However, as I planned for my role at the event, I began to wonder how I could possibly portray all the fine qualities that I saw in this person and began to pay particular attention to why it was that I felt this way. Over the next week or so, I began to take more notice of the way he interacted with others in the office, the way he displayed leadership qualities, and the way he went about everyday things.

By the time our great performance came around, I had learned a lot more about my mentor — just by taking notice of the little things. While I had always admired his leadership style, I had never really

continued on next page

taken the time to understand why. By watching him in action in day-to-day activities, I learned even more from my mentor (and came up with some good material for the skit).

During the team skit, the impersonation of my mentor went well. The entire team had a good laugh, my mentor was flattered (and a bit embarrassed), and I had fun with it. At the end I had learned not only to look up and connect with people I admire, but to really take the time to understand why—for that is where the real learning can take place!

Robyn Brown, Stanton Chase:

My mentor Carol and I both worked in an international corporation and met at a development seminar. Over the years our professional relationship developed as we were thrown together to work on the development of methodologies and tools that could be used globally. These instances were often random, involved coming together for a few short days with other global team members and then returning to our local offices to churn out results, whilst also holding down day jobs with demanding clients. Carol provided valuable coaching to me on my work and insights into how to present or develop ideas or concepts, challenged my thinking, and, on the long flights home, gave me a lot to think about.

The real value of this mentoring relationship climaxed some five years later, when I was having some really serious difficulties with "Jerry," one of the more senior executives in our local organization. He was determined to remove me from his team and used underhanded and bullying tactics as his weapons. I called Carol to discuss this with her, and she was most supportive and helpful in how best to deal with the issue. Unknown to me, Jerry had respect for Carol's technical skills in my area of expertise and asked her to visit and conduct a review of the work of my area. She conducted this review in a most professional manner. She highlighted to Jerry the real issues—his shortcomings as a leader, including lack of support, poor team cohesion, and deliberate undermining of the contribution of team members.

I truly valued Carol's mentoring—I had learned a lot, way beyond development of technical skills. She helped me to pluck myself from the day-to-day mire and to gain insights into other people's motivations and how they perceived my contribution. I also observed at close hand a true professional in action — something I genuinely reflect on often now in my new profession.

John Porcari, Five Star Development:
I was working on a tough engagement where we were attempting to enact some significant transformational change in a very stoic industry. Unsurprisingly, the environment was highly politically charged, and I stepped into the crosshairs of a senior vice president who had forced the dismissal of other project team members who had exposed some unhealthy work practices in his area of responsibility. Having taken pride in adding as much high value as I could throughout my entire career, I was deeply troubled when I was told this SVP was questioning my value and wanted me removed from the project. I took this very hard, as I felt that everything I had done in this client setting was entirely appropriate and was needed to ensure the success of the project. Needless to say, the situation had shaken my confidence a good deal, and my impact was suffering as a result.

Fortunately, a partner who was a mentor to me was in town for a quality assurance review. We were going through some of the tactical aspects of the project over lunch, when he asked me how I was doing. "Fine," I said, continuing to move down the list of topics we needed to cover. Sensing that I was not totally fine, he said, "Let's put the list down and talk about how you are really doing. What's going on?" As I looked at him, I knew that this was a man who was sincerely concerned about me and the impact of my distraction, so I shared the situation with him. While I was finishing, he smiled and said, "You've never gotten threatened to be removed from a job before?" (as if this were a desirable right of passage about which one should be proud).

He then continued, "John, if you have not seriously ruffled some senior executive's feathers before, you may not have been giving the client the best value for their dollar. Our clients pay us a lot of money to get big results — and you can't get big results without making some entrenched

continued on next page

people pretty uncomfortable. So congratulations—and stop worrying! We believe in you and what you are doing. No one is going to look down upon you, and, if anyone does, let me know and I will set them straight." As I let all that sink in, a big smile grew on my face. I had let my perceptions of how others viewed the situation cloud my confidence in my actions. But, in taking that risk, I had gained a great reward. I just did not know it until my mentor helped to frame it in a different way!

The outcome? Well, I did not get removed from that job. My mentor helped me to recognize that the best successes in work (and life) have risk as a primary ingredient. Having pulled back and recognized the unhealthy patterns of the SVP, knowing that what I was candidly pushing was entirely appropriate, *and* knowing that I was appreciated and supported by my mentor and others for doing so helped me to have the courage to stick to my convictions—regardless of the consequences. That was ten years ago. That company is doing worlds better than they were back then, and that SVP is long gone. What has remained in me is that valuable mentoring experience. I have made it a point to share this experience with all of my mentees over the years to free them from the fear of not taking smart risks. I believe that they have also benefited from the time my mentor invested in me (as will others who they mentor along the way).

Lisa Riether, Accenture:
I ask all of those that I mentor or counsel to draft a timeline relative to their career roles, development, milestones, etc. I have seen everything from a formal document done using Visio software to a timeline done in pencil on the back of napkin. Creating the timeline requires the mentees to really think forward about their careers while reflecting on their past. The timeline is a single-page illustration of their career journey, future goals, milestone timeline, and actions they need to take to create the next opportunity. As a mentor, I have found this to lead to meaningful and insightful discussions with mentees.

One of the most insightful moments I had was during a discussion with a mentee who took her timeline forward just 12 to 16 months. She looked up at me and said, "I stopped at this point because I am not sure I see myself pursuing the next level here as I may go back to school or do something else." While the six-year company veteran inside of me sent my mind spinning ("Oh, she is a short-timer; she is not committed to staying here; maybe she is considering leaving. Should she really show her intent, or should she revise her timeline to send the right message to the supervisors with whom she will share this?"), the mentor in me realized two things:

- She had just trusted me with her honest view. I needed to both honor the trust she had placed in me and recognize the honesty so she would know that she had support for whatever she decided to do.
- Her next role may determine if we lose or keep her as an employee.

I opted to respond to her by reassuring her that her illustration was fine and that she would have my support for her and her career decisions both inside and outside of Accenture. I also mentioned that while I hoped she might find future roles to provide her with opportunities to remain with Accenture, I certainly understood exploring other options, including school. We discussed how she might handle sharing her timeline with her supervisors in a way that she need not disclose her uncertainty, but simply focus the discussion on what her short-term goals and milestones were, because this was most relevant to them anyway.

I have often reflected on this conversation as an example of the role a mentor plays as a trusted advisor. As I was not her direct supervisor, there was no career implication to her sharing this information with me. Also, it gave her insight and coaching on how to position herself honestly without sending the message that she is uncertain or focused on pursuing other options outside of the company.

Galvanize Your Team

Once you pull together the members of your board of directors and obtain their input on the direction of your vision, you're well on your way to making it a reality. What else can you do to expedite your journey?

And as a mentor, know that investing in people is one of the most valuable investments you'll ever make. Although the return on investment (ROI) may be hard to measure, the people in your life will have the greatest impact on you. How do you invest in people? Pay attention to them! People don't want to "do a job"—they want to be on a team! So make them feel like they're an important part of your team, and you'll get more from them than you could ever get through any other means. Having long-term, trust-based, productive relationships will contribute more to the quality of your life than anything else.

As a mentee, you need someone on your side to be an advocate for you—to get that assignment, that new job, that promotion, or whatever. Make sure you have a mentor or other team member who is that advocate for you. And don't forget, it's up to you to actively seek advice and feedback. This will demonstrate to you and your team that you have the ability to receive and process constructive feedback, and the initiative and maturity to take steps to improve yourself and your performance as a result.

Why waste any time worrying whether or not you're on the right track? Have a heart-to-heart with your mentor or other team members who are in a position to know this, and ask!

CHAPTER 3 RECAP

LESSON #7: **Identify the members of your board of directors.**
LESSON #8: **Know how to use your team.**
LESSON #9: **Find your mentors and team members.**

ACTION ITEMS:

- Given that the most important people in your professional life are your mentors, develop a list of who they are, what role they play (particular areas of focus), and why they are important to you.
- If you don't have a mentor, begin to look for one. This person should be someone you trust and who will give you feedback on your performance and help you get more responsibilities and perhaps even a promotion.
- Based on your vision, who might you want to include on your "team?" Some suggestions: an industry or functional leader, a peer to help with the political environment and some of the issues you might be facing, and someone from outside your work environment to give you a different perspective.
- Begin to talk to your mentor about your vision goals, and a proposed timeline. The purpose is to define your long-term goals (for example, to be one of the top HR professionals in three to five years and to achieve the next promotion level in one to two years) and then to review the interim goals, roles, and responsibilities needed to make this happen. This information will help you to develop a more detailed plan (which we will address in the next chapter).

REFLECT AND RECORD:

- Given the vision you've already developed for You, Inc., what are the qualities and skills of the players you need on your team? Who are the people already on your team?
- Remember, good leaders develop their successors so they can take on more responsibilities and work toward their next promotion.

-4-

DEVELOP YOUR PLAN

"Failing to plan is planning to fail."
—ALAN LAKEIN

Through my consulting experience, I've learned that having a detailed implementation plan is the most effective way to achieve any significant objective. After all, you would never head out on a road trip without both a destination and a map to get you there. Your destination is your vision for You, Inc. and your implementation plan maps out the way you plan to get there.

The basic concept behind strategizing and planning is one of *prioritization*. No one has unlimited time and resources. Therefore, the question is, how are you going to make the most out of *yours?* Even the wealthiest person on earth is limited to the same 24 hours a day, 168 hours a week.

Choosing and carefully planning how to invest your time and resources is one of the most important determinations you will ever make.

Your plan should be more than a mere "to do" list. It should stay aligned with your vision and require frequent feedback from your team to ensure that it is efficient and in keeping with your desired results. Beginning with the end in mind, your plan should provide clear and precise steps with deadlines that will take you from where you are today to where you want to be tomorrow.

Why Have a Plan?

A plan keeps you on track; it keeps you motivated. And, most importantly, it is a tool that ensures you are making the choices *you* want to be making rather than veering in directions *others* may want you to take.

Also, developing a plan prompts you to provide much-needed specificity to the goal you developed for You, Inc.—that is, what "the end in mind" really looks like and exactly what it is going to take to achieve it.

And, it's critical to ensure that your goal is achievable. The amount of time and effort required to achieve your vision may not become clear to you until you have enumerated the specific steps it will take to accomplish it. Once you have planned out your steps, confirm your intended approach and your targeted time frame with key members of your team. They may tell you that it's just not realistic to plan on getting promoted in your first two years. Or, that if you want to become a museum curator, you better include foreign language lessons in your plan, as major museums require fluency in at least three.

Write your plan down. Having defined steps, deliverables, and delivery dates will provide you with a document you can use to review your progress. Just like a corporate CEO, it is essential to write out your plan because this is how you begin to both internalize and communicate it: by describing what you want to do and what you need to do to accomplish your goal. (Besides, it looks more official in print!) And, once you internalize it, you begin making it happen.

Set Your Sights High

When I first started with Accenture, I had no idea how long I would be there. I was glad to have a "job," but I certainly didn't see it as the thirty-six-year career it turned out to be. I primarily did what people asked me to do. Looking back, I regret not maximizing my experiences during those earlier years of my career. I didn't work toward developing the specific skills and capabilities necessary to get to my first promotion in two years, to manager in six and partner in twelve to fourteen. I learned an important lesson during that time: to be able to make an impact and be successful professionally, I must shift my thinking from "having a job" to "building a career."

I remember a time when I was talking with a group of newly matriculated MBA students and asked them what they hoped to accomplish over the next two years. One of them thought it was pretty obvious because they were there to get an MBA. However, another replied that she wanted to prepare to take on management responsibility in the automotive industry.

The latter MBA candidate, with her ideal vision in mind, clearly had interim goals she wanted to achieve over the subsequent two years beyond simply earning her MBA. These included landing an internship with an automotive company. To accomplish this goal, some of her tasks were identifying and taking the right courses that would provide her with the skills necessary to land her ideal job. She also wanted to learn about successful careers in the industry, identify people in the industry, and determine how she could meet them.

Rather than letting things happen to her, this business student knew what she wanted and set specific interim goals that would help her achieve her dream. Step-by-step, she built her own ladder with the hope of ultimately getting to the executive suite. This is exactly the mind-set that all individuals should adopt to survive, as well as thrive, in a world that is characterized by constant change.

Your life is yours to live, and your goals are yours to make real. If you don't go to the trouble of making a comprehensive implementation plan, you'll more easily fall victim to whatever happens to come your way. And that might be something very different from what you want. Why not choose to maximize one of the most valuable assets of your life: your 365 days a year? You will be able to accomplish more through setting an ambitious plan, even if you fall short of it, than you will if you don't set your sights high in the first place. So set your sights high, and go for it.

Reevaluating Your Plan

Your plan may not be static. In fact, it may change dramatically over time. For this reason, you must be vigilant and honest with yourself about what your goals really are. If your goals change, your plan will become a moving target that requires tweaking along the way.

A good example of this is a plan I set in motion over a decade ago to be on the board of trustees of Purdue University. At that time, I had not developed my vision of creating positive change for women. I was interested in making Purdue the best educational institution it could be.

When a vacancy on the board became available due to a retirement, I jumped at the chance to be voted in. Without reevaluating my goals, which had changed over the course of eleven years, I held on tight to the idea that I wanted to be on the board of trustees and did what I thought was necessary to make it happen. Up to this time, the track record of the Purdue Alumni Association (PAA) Board nominating a woman was not good—it had never done so. After the presentations of the four candidates (including myself) at the PAA board meeting, they nominated another man. Some seemed to think that my speech was off-putting, although I was also told that if a man had given it, it would have been considered very good. They were just not ready for a diverse candidate.

In the end, the decision has turned out to be helpful for my longer range plans. Given the vision of my institute to "impact zillions of women and girls," being on the board would have taken time away from making this happen. Now I have more time to bring about diversity in academic institutions, to make them a great place to work for women, as well as affect women's lives in other arenas.

The Critical Components of Your Plan

Implementing your vision means considering the details of the requirements to bring your goal to life. What kinds of skills, experiences, and knowledge will it entail? In terms of applying the MIH Model to your own life, making your plan is about asking yourself: who am I today, and who do I need to become to accomplish my goals? What are the steps I need to take to move from today to tomorrow?

To prepare a sufficiently detailed implementation plan, you should start by doing the following:

- ◆ Have a clear definition of your vision or goal.
- ◆ Keep in mind your current skills, capabilities, and experiences, and define those you believe you will need to have to achieve your goal.
- ◆ Enumerate sequentially and define clearly the tasks necessary for you to achieve your goal, as well as how you will know when you are finished (deliverables) and when you expect to complete each step along the way (due dates).
- ◆ Identify the team members who will help you make your dream happen, and ensure that their expectations are in line with your own.
- ◆ Given the input you receive from your team, refine and add detail to your plan.
- ◆ Set interim goals and schedule review sessions (both independently, and with members of your advisory team) to ensure that you are making progress toward achieving your goal.
- ◆ Write the due dates in your calendar, and block out the time needed to complete the necessary work.

Break It Down Into Steps

Now, let's consider being even more specific. The best way to approach your goal may be to define the tasks in more detailed steps, each having its own deadline for accomplishment. Anyone wanting to run a marathon doesn't simply muster all their will and head outdoors that very day to run 26.2 miles without stopping. You need a comprehensive plan and a team to help you—and your body must be conditioned well in advance in order to run the marathon's distance.

Don't fall into the "New Year's Day Syndrome" of aiming for an entirely changed life overnight. That's a sure recipe for failure and disappointment. Just as "small strokes fell a great oak," each small step will take you closer to your eventual goal.

Set your expectations realistically, and be patient with yourself. If you begin a weightlifting program to tone your muscles, you won't likely see any difference after the first session. But lift weights every other day, and in a few short weeks you will notice a measurable difference—one that can eventually require you to drop a size! In any case, it makes you feel better.

Phrase Your Plan to Motivate You

It's far more motivating to operate from a place of "I want" than "I should." For example, when launching an exercise program, what's more likely to have you looking forward to going out for your walk: "I should walk two miles every day, even though I hate walking" or "I want to lose weight, so I want to walk two miles every day?" Better yet, "I love to walk and feel physically fit, so much that I want to give myself that pleasure every day!" Create an image of the outcome you desire that is so appealing it won't possibly let you fail.

It's also far more motivating to make things as pleasurable for yourself as possible. If one of your goals for professional development includes reading two books a month, yet you find reading to be a chore, why not invest in a tape player and headphones so that you can listen to books on tape instead? Or, if you also enjoy learning through interacting with others as part of a group, perhaps you could make your goal attending two seminars or talks every month, which would also allow you to enjoy the social setting.

Revisit Your Plan Regularly

Making the time to develop and revise your plan for achieving your vision for your life is as important as living it. Otherwise, it is all too easy to get caught up in what *other* people want you to do rather than what you *yourself* want to do. Make a commitment to yourself to plan your life, and to live your plan. As CEO of You, Inc., you should set up your planning sessions—annually, quarterly, weekly, even daily. Don't leave the trajectory of your life to chance! Rather, think carefully about what's most important to you, and how you can achieve it.

Here are some ideas to help keep you on track:

- ◆ Schedule your planning sessions in your date book, and give them the same high priority you'd give your best client or an important project.
- ◆ Devote a couple of days a year to planning the coming year, ideally during October to get it ready for January 1. Spend time reviewing the prior two years, understanding what you accomplished and what you didn't. What does your recent evaluation tell you about your progress toward your goals and your areas for improvement? Additionally, what went right with your plan, and what went wrong? This information will be critical to how you will update your vision (if necessary), and the related implementation plan. Don't forget to meet with your mentors and those helpful to your career development to make sure that your expectations are still in alignment with theirs.

And then:

- ◆ Devote quality time each quarter, checking in on your progress over the past quarter and planning for the next quarter.
- ◆ Devote at least an hour every week to review your week and plan your coming week.
- ◆ Devote some time every morning or evening to reviewing the prior day and planning the next.
- ◆ Determine whether something has happened to affect your goal or your plan, and make corrections accordingly.

Again, it's important to take these sessions seriously, and to occasionally get away from your office, your computer, and your telephone to have uninterrupted time with yourself. Get up before your family, or slip out for a *latte* in the afternoon—whatever you have to do to get away to have time for yourself. (And turn your cell phone off—this is not catch-up time, but time for you to reflect on yourself and You, Inc. No multitasking!) A friend of mine calls this thinking time, and I call it time to listen to myself. It's amazing what you can learn. As an example, the subtitle for this book came to me when I was driving along, with no interruptions. I had an opportunity to listen to myself, and the words came to me out of the blue.

This may sound like a lot of planning, but out of fifty-two weeks a year, don't you have to admit it's worth it to invest roughly two weeks (spread out over the course of the year) to ensure that you're getting everything you want out of the other fifty weeks?

Integrating Your Dreams with Reality

So, now you've got your vision, and you've made your plan. But what you also have is a job. Your vision of winning the 2036 U.S. presidential race does not change the fact that, at present, you're a summer intern on the Hill. How do you integrate your present-day responsibilities into your strategy for a future goal? The answer: use each day to propel yourself toward your goal.

You must excel at your current work to achieve the goals you set for yourself. For instance, one of my mentees aspired to be rewarded with a promotion. She felt overwhelmed by her daily tasks and unable to focus on how to get promoted. My question to her was, "Who is going to help make sure it happens for you? That is, who is your advocate at the table to say, 'Of course she should be promoted because she has been doing the job for the last year.'"

Then I asked how the person with the power to promote her would know that she had been doing so well. For example, was her client talking about how great she was and how much value she was delivering? Was she visible to the industry team, and did they see her as someone who was performing in the role to which she aspired? If not, why not? She needed to make sure her expectations of what she thought she needed to do and the expectations of the people promoting her were the same. Her responsibilities, and the value she delivered to both her clients and to her company, were all going to be instrumental in the decision regarding her promotion.

The mentee decided that the only way to get the attention of her superiors was to go the extra mile with each project to which she was assigned. If she found a task to be dull, she put an extra sheen on it. If it was a team project, she made sure to speak up in meetings to become visible to those who could promote her. All of this work actually made her present job—the one she was trying to leave behind—more exciting because the job had become more than an end in itself. It was a stepping-stone to the promotion that, of course, she was eventually rewarded.

As this example illustrates, in order to achieve your goal, you have to not only excel in your daily activities, but you also can't be shy about it. Women especially need to be aware of their tendency to make other people look good without necessarily getting the credit for making things happen behind the scenes. This is a tightrope to walk: How aggressive do you need to be—or feel comfortable being—in letting people know about your talents and accomplishments? The answer will depend on your personality as well as where you are in your life. Think about it and see whether you need to turn it up or down a notch. And again, ask a mentor for guidance.

★ ★ ★

Your implementation plan must take your daily responsibilities into account. But more importantly, it should *take advantage* of your daily tasks. Each day is an opportunity to take steps toward your goal. If you get bogged down, escape for a few minutes of thinking time to get a bird's-eye view of your life. Take a dispassionate look at your tasks and see if there's a way to delegate them. Or, even better, go the extra mile with the project and show a superior how brilliant you are!

I hope Part I of this book has brought to light the importance of laying the necessary groundwork for You, Inc. Once you have your vision, team, and plan in place, you will be ready to *take action*. Part II will be your guide as you navigate your journey as CEO of You, Inc. The lessons in the following pages were learned the hard way: through trial and error. As your virtual mentor, my greatest wish is that by including them here, your journey to success will be smooth sailing.

CHAPTER 4 RECAP

LESSON #10: Create the plan to achieve your vision.
LESSON #11: Set your sights high.
LESSON #12: Integrate your dreams with reality.

ACTION ITEMS:

- Using the information developed in the previous chapters, create the tasks that you will need to complete to achieve your goals. Each task or step should have an outcome and a due date.
- Ensure that you are doing something to help you move toward achieving your goals every day. For example, do your daily tasks in a way that is recognized by your supervisor as exceptional; ask for more responsibilities (if you have time for them) to expand your skill development; and ask for continuous feedback so you know how you are progressing.
- Make time in your schedule for your planning sessions. They should be daily, monthly, and yearly.

REFLECT AND RECORD:

- Take an honest look at how you have reached your goals in the past. Are you a planner by nature, or do you generally take life as it comes?
- If the latter applies, how will you change your habits to incorporate more planning?

PART II

Navigating the Journey

-5-

THE PROCESS OF NAVIGATING

"A journey of a thousand miles begins with a single step."
—CHINESE PROVERB

n addition to developing a vision for You, Inc., a plan, and a supportive board of directors, you are also responsible for navigating the daily journey of You, Inc. This will involve conducting the day-to-day operations of You, Inc., as well as continually evaluating your performance to see if you are on the right track.

Navigating your journey will require an array of marketing, communication, financial, and people skills that will help you achieve your goals. Just like any other project you have tackled, you have work to do and deadlines to meet in order to succeed. And, of course, you have your team who will continue to advise and counsel you throughout this process. With this final—and vital—step in the Make-It-Happen Model, I will show you how to go about developing essential skills you need to successfully run You, Inc.

Taking Action to Make Your Vision a Reality

In the previous chapters, I discussed the first steps toward creating change: envisioning the future, building your team, and developing your plan. Now, it's time to *take action*. Using initiative—getting yourself comfortable with the idea that results can, and do, start with you—is a form of self-leadership. This is your chance to embrace your role as CEO and become the leader you need to be to realize your dreams.

Taking action is the key to turning any idea into a reality. And, in this case, the idea is what you have envisioned for You, Inc. However, many people have lots of ideas—occasionally, even a brilliant one that they don't implement.

Why is it so hard sometimes to take action? We can *feel* our ambition. We know we have the ability to *do* something. Yet between our ambitions and our abilities, sometimes another *A* word can creep in: ambivalence, which occurs when our focus is destroyed by conflicting feelings about a particular goal. Ambivalence typically is rooted in fear. It's when we say to ourselves, "Yes, I want to get more physically fit, but I've been feeling too tired to go for a walk every day." Or, "Yes, I want to take that new job, but I'm not sure I have what it takes to excel in such a powerful position."

These fears, whether unfounded or not, can seriously hinder the growth of You, Inc. You have the power to overcome them by continually enacting the process I will describe in the following paragraphs. And always remember, you've built a team you can depend on. If you feel ambivalence or fear creep in, talk to your mentor, colleague, or advisor for a much-needed confidence boost.

The Process of Navigating

Navigating your journey has three important overriding components: determining your progress; recognizing your roadblocks; and recharting your course.

Locate Your Current Position Relative to Your Goal (Determine Your Progress)

While you take action, you'll need to determine your progress along the way. Did your actions have the intended results? Are you behind, ahead of, or right on schedule with where you thought you would be? How do the resources you expended (such as time, energy, money) stack up against the planned budgets and the results that you've achieved?

Let's take buying a house as an example. Perhaps you planned on saving $15,000 for a down payment on a house within twelve months—and you've just determined that after four months, you've only managed to save $3,000. So, despite your intentions (of reducing your cost of living and increasing your savings), in one-third of the time you've allotted to reach your goal, you are not even a quarter of the way there. This should send up a red flag.

As you proceed with your journey, it's important to constantly evaluate how you are progressing. Not doing so can get you offtrack and keep you from realizing your goals as efficiently as you would like. Also, keep in regular contact with the members of your board of directors. This is one way to continue to confirm the accuracy of your plan or to know how to revise it when necessary.

What "Roadblocks" Caused You a Delay?

Because of all the variables in life, it's rare that you'll be exactly where you thought you'd be exactly when you thought you'd be there. Whenever there's a discrepancy between where you are and where you thought you'd be, analyze the underlying causes of this variance so you can address them. Perhaps you faced unanticipated obstacles, either external (for example, a change in the market, the debut of a competitor, or the lack of productivity of a teammate) or internal (such as your own lack of experience, or hindered productivity due to lack of confidence or health issues).

For example, a highly respected leader at Accenture once said that everyone should receive a less-than-average evaluation once in their life. I concur because it happened to me. This experience, although a particularly humbling roadblock, can be one of the most significant lessons of your career.

What did I do in this situation? I looked at myself in the mirror and said, "Susan, you are talented and have ambitious goals. You need to understand this situation, do what you need to do, and move on." (In the next chapter, I'll talk more about becoming a feedback addict.)

The key is to get over the problem and get on with making improvements. Don't wear the roadblock on your sleeve for too long—or else you risk people thinking they made the right decision, and your opportunity for correction will be gone.

Ask the person who presented you with the problem to help you solve it. And, be sure that you understand the problem clearly, so you know what to fix. While humbling, if you have the maturity to grow from the feedback you receive, these can be invaluable turning points in your career.

Rechart Your Course As Necessary

As the CEO of You, Inc., it's essential for you to monitor where you are in relation to your planned milestones and targeted timeline. As you encounter unanticipated events, determine whether adjustments must be made to your plans, milestones, and target dates.

Don't allow roadblocks to throw you off course. It can be difficult to bounce back emotionally once we stumble. At such times, additional support from your team may help to build your confidence and give you perspective. Pick yourself back up and shake off doldrums and negative thinking. Building emotional strength over time will help you navigate your journey more effectively.

Make sure you objectively analyze any missteps and move forward a bit wiser from their lessons. Adjust your plans to take these lessons into consideration.

Remember: learn, adjust, and move forward.

★ ★ ★

"All that is necessary to break the spell of inertia and frustration is this: Act as if it were impossible to fail."

—DOROTHEA BRANDE

Making the right adjustments along the way can be tricky. But, it is often the case that the roadblocks you face eventually lead to progress. I learned this painful lesson years ago while working in Accenture's Houston office. My peers were promoted to the manager level, while I was passed over. I was dumbfounded—not to mention disappointed and embarrassed. What did they have that I didn't?

What they had was business expertise, while my focus was more technical. As it turns out, a few weeks later my then-husband was transferred to Chicago. I asked for a transfer back to Accenture's Chicago office and got the OK—as well as a promotion to manager. Why? Because my skills were found to fit a manager role in Chicago, which was a much larger office with a greater need for my technical expertise.

The difference between the two offices was an external factor that affected my goal of being promoted. Still, that experience led me to make a shift in my goals: I needed to become more than a technical manager. I hadn't seen anyone move higher in the organization with only technical skills. I immediately decided to set my goals on getting more business-related projects. I had to develop a strategy to break out of my technical roles and to begin working on the business functions of my clients. As a result, I began to look at my peers to determine what experiences I needed to have and then proactively looked to develop those same opportunities for myself. I then adjusted my plan and created an opportunity to shift my course to achieve my vision.

★ ★ ★

If you approach managing You, Inc. with confidence and vigilance, the possibilities are limitless. You are at the helm, weaving through all of the obstacles in your way to eventually reach your potential. After all the preparation and planning, navigating the journey of You, Inc. will be an exciting time—a time for you to show your skills and talents to the world.

CHAPTER 5 RECAP

LESSON #13: Take action to make your vision a reality.
LESSON #14: Know where you are in relation to where you planned to be.
LESSON #15: Learn from roadblocks, adjust your plan, and move forward.

ACTION ITEMS:

- ◆ Use your thinking time to help you realize the progress that you are making. On a weekly basis, note the actions that you complete and congratulate yourself for accomplishing them.
- ◆ Recognize your successes. Build your confidence.

REFLECT AND RECORD:

- ◆ Look back over your journal to see evidence of your progress. If there is a difference between where you planned to be and where you ended up, think about the reasons why.
- ◆ Were certain tasks not completed due to lack of focus? Were you too aggressive in your plans? Were there unexpected tasks to get done?
- ◆ Forgive and forget. As the saying goes, forgiveness is a gift you give yourself. Don't put a wall between you and those you may perceive to have put a roadblock in your path.
- ◆ What did you learn this week? Adjust your plans and move forward to next week.

-6-

THE MARKETABILITY OF YOU, INC.

"You are unique, and if that is not fulfilled, then something has been lost."
—MARTHA GRAHAM

A key decision every CEO must make is to decide how to best present the company to the marketplace. What product does it offer? Is it competitive? How can it market itself most effectively? To further enhance the reputation of You, Inc. it is absolutely essential that you think of yourself in these terms. After all, the world is a competitive place. What is it about You, Inc. that is unique or valuable? What are your skills and capabilities? Why should a company (your customer) recruit or retain your product versus others that are in the pipeline? How do you set yourself apart?

The most important resources at You, Inc. are your "product," or skills and capabilities, and the external "package" that presents those capabilities.

Think of Yourself as Both a Product and a Commercial

What is your product? Essentially, it is you. It may be the fact that you are good in marketing or that you have the necessary skills needed for the job or that you have the potential to be an exceptional performer. Whatever it is, there is a way to sell it to your customer. Over the course of your life and career, you will put yourself "out there" in a variety of situations in which others will not know who you are. What will get their attention? How will you make a positive, lasting impression?

If you have a product to be marketed, you need your customers to compensate you for your product. You need to keep them coming back for your services because your product is always relevant to them and the marketplace. By achieving a long product lifespan, you will remain relevant.

Does your product keep pace with the changes of the marketplace you are in? Or, are you lagging behind? Think proactively about the state of the marketplace and how you can best position yourself to take advantage of every opportunity. If you make your decisions with an eye on the future, you will make your career progression happen *for* you, not let it happen *to* you.

Like any other brand, people need to know and remember your name. One way to do this is to create a positive tagline for yourself by making what you say so memorable that it forges a positive connection with the listener. Every successful product needs to become known to the world, including You, Inc. This takes skill, will, and an understanding of how to communicate your message—your tagline—in different settings and circumstances. Your message should be consistent yet customized for the various audiences you address.

For example, at a conference, introducing yourself to new people one-on-one is different from introducing yourself at a group table at lunch, which is different still from introducing yourself as a speaker to the assembled group of conference attendees. Each instance requires a brief introduction of who you are and what you do and for whom. In the first case, your focus would be on creating a personal connection. This connection would be physically expressed with eye contact and a firm handshake. Additionally, you would connect by exploring shared interests that could possibly spark a mutual bond.

When introducing yourself to groups, you still want to maintain the physical connection through eye contact and good posture, but your ideas will have to be broader because they should interest more than one party. When addressing a group table, you will be able to connect with your audience by creating a dialogue with those at your table. This give-and-take can be dynamic and a good opportunity to expose your "product" to the group. The same advantages can apply when speaking to a large group, but your message will reach even further. As always, your delivery should be succinct and relevant, without being dry.

You are the same product, but within a thirty-minute span, you may need the flexibility to be effective one-on-one, one-on-ten, and one-on-hundreds. For your product to be memorable, you need to have the skill and versatility to promote yourself appropriately.

Speak Up to Stand Out

There's a modern-day adage (most often attributed to Xerox's Alan Kay) that states: "having a new point of view is worth 80 IQ points." Without quibbling over whether that's an accurate assessment of exactly how much smarter people will perceive you to be when you offer an opinion, the gist of his comment is true: having a point of view is important—just as important is your willingness to share it.

In one of my annual performance reviews, I was told that I should speak up in every meeting I attended, or people would wonder why I was there. I took this advice to heart and learned that how I communicate my point of view is just as important as having one.

Make it a point to practice speaking up—in meetings, at conferences, wherever you have the opportunity. Then, ask someone you trust for feedback. Were you on target? Did you make your point effectively? Listen to their advice and counsel.

Remember: it's not always a matter of being "right." In many cases, there's not a clear "right" answer but rather a range of informed opinions on a subject, both pro and con. That said, you should also be in sync with your team's point of view. Even if your personal point of view differs at first, it's crucial to eventually get on board with your team's message—or else find another team. If you are on the "right" team (which could be defined as one in which your point of view counts), it will certainly enhance your chances of achieving success.

One of the most important things aspiring women executives can do is improve their communication style. By speaking up fearlessly and commanding your audience's attention, you will make your point effectively. Know what your point or question is, and make it or ask it succinctly.

A common reality for women and communication is not being heard, or being "talked over" by others at the table. I used to worry about this. Did I say something wrong? Was it not said clearly? The sad truth is that it can happen that your audience is not ready to listen to you. An aspiring woman's good idea can fall flat while the man across the table expresses—and gets credit for—that very same thought. As frustrating as this is, don't take it personally. People have a tendency to accept ideas and comments from different people for all sorts of reasons. However, you may want to find a way to let someone know when it happens.

At the Podium

For most of us, there comes a time in our professional lives when we must address a large audience. Public speaking tends to instill fear in even the bravest among us. I've seen highly respected professional men and women sweat and shake before having to give a speech. Many will readily admit that public speaking ranks as a top fear in life.

We've all been witness to public speaking disasters over the course of our lives: endless commencement addresses, forgotten speeches, and inappropriate jokes. A colleague of mine told me her particular horror story after watching an old video of herself giving a speech. It seems that while addressing a large group of colleagues, her younger, nervous self used improper language several times in an attempt to get laughs. She watched the tape in dismay, belatedly blushing.

More recently, a woman announcing her candidacy for the U.S. Senate misplaced a page of her speech in the midst of the announcement. The press had a field day!

Fortunately, there are strategies you can employ to avoid such a disaster. You must ensure that you are really prepared. One of the most important ways is to do what we have all been told: practice. I've found a direct correlation between preparation time and delivery ease. I see far too many people winging it. Don't be one of them. After all, this is a great marketing opportunity and a chance to present your product to a wide audience.

Below are some ideas that can help you establish a reputation as an effective public speaker:

- **Know your material.** If you are reading your speech, you will not be able to engage your audience. It's fine to have notes to refer to, but commit your main points to memory. Know what you want to say, and talk to the audience.
- **Punch it up.** Don't let your speech be too dry. Back up factual information with stories and visual images to support your thesis. Humor can also be a tool to keep listeners focused on you.
- **Avoid wardrobe malfunctions.** Wear the clothes you feel most confident and comfortable in. Don't "debut" a new dress or jacket on the day of your speech. Choose a classic item that you know makes you look and feel your best.
- **Time it.** Know how much time your speech takes, and leave time to interact with the audience during a Q&A session.

Develop Your Product with an Eye toward the Future

You should include the never-ending pursuit of product excellence as part of your career strategy. It's critical that you jump at opportunities to enhance what you can offer to the market. For me, this meant building a solid technology base early on, supplemented with business skills as I grew with the company. When I saw new technologies like SAP emerging, I developed the technical and change management skills to meet my clients' needs. When I saw globalization advancing, I sought positions that would provide me opportunities to work in different cultural environments around the world.

To keep your product marketable, always look for opportunities that will build a good foundation for your progression over the course of your career. It may be helpful to look at your peers to see what they are learning. In addition to developing industry expertise, you should understand such things as the niche your company occupies, how the work you are doing affects the company's bottom line, and where the company is moving over the next few years.

Packaging You, Inc.

> *"You there—you don't have a look. Get one."*
>
> —MARIA CALLAS TO A STUDENT,
> IN TERRENCE MCNALLY'S PLAY *MASTER CLASS*

First impressions are a fact of life. In business, first impressions are critically important for women aspiring to leadership positions. That's why it's crucial to heed the advice that Maria Callas pointedly offers an aspiring star in the play *Master Class*.

I've seen ambitious professionals, in their drive to get ahead, make the mistake of focusing more on upgrading their "product" than on improving the "package" through which they present those competencies to the world. Don't forget that a person's first encounter with you will be based on first seeing your package and then receiving a product demonstration (that is, hearing what comes out of your mouth).

You need to package your product just like any other product on the market. Pay as much attention to your physical package as brand managers pay to their own products' presentation. Strike a balance between coming up with a look that represents you, yet is appropriate to the culture of your company and industry, while also allowing you to stand out in the marketplace.

Envision politicians getting ready for a political debate. Of course they bone up on the issues likely to be discussed, and commit to memory the key facts necessary to argue their positions. However, in addition to that, their most important preparations are likely to include bringing in an image consultant to advise on what they should wear (in terms of styles, colors, etc.) to enhance their authority or sincerity or whatever trait they most wish to project, as well as a speech coach to work with them on their delivery.

It's difficult to provide general guidance on this topic because everyone must eventually find the right answer for herself. However, based on my experience, I feel every woman should embrace her own style and individuality within the generally accepted norm of her company and industry. Dress for the position you want within your organization.

Dressing for success will depend on the specific culture of the organization in which you work. If it's a bank in New York or London, you will probably wear a black or blue suit. An advertising agency, on the other hand, has a completely different set of rules. In the more creative environment, you would be expected to be more in tune with fashion trends and dress accordingly. Be sure to check the dress code before you arrive at the meeting, conference, or your first day at work.

The difficulty women face in today's workplace is the fact that dress codes tend to be unspoken. In most cases, there will not be a hard and fast "you must come to work wearing a conservative suit in either black, gray, or navy." On the contrary, the rules of the game may be just that, but they go unsaid. This leaves us guessing, and guessing incorrectly can have serious implications for one's career advancement.

The surest way to solve this dilemma involves three steps:

1. Observe your colleagues. Who is getting ahead? How are they perceived? Are they the more conservatively dressed, or do they take risks?
2. Choose sophistication over trend. Always err on the side of conservative polish rather than fleeting trends that may not be appropriate for your body type.

Professional Image in the Workplace: Is It Important?

By Maureen Costello, MA, CIP Principal of Image Launch
(www.imagelaunch.com)

Women often approach me at networking events and whisper the halting question "Does a professional image at work really matter?" The short answer is yes. People react to us based on their perceptions. And they are more likely to do business with us if we look the part.

So, why does a professional image matter? The biggest reason is that without a professional look, your promotional opportunities are limited. Whether you care about advancement or not, your reputation is at stake. One of my client's over-alluring looks and suggestive wardrobe set her back because the senior manager never provided the exposure she needed in high-visibility meetings. She was an object of intrigue rather than substance.

Another client wore tight-fitting, high-fashion garb that disqualified her from higher-level meetings abroad. But once she raised her level of sophistication, selected better color choices and higher quality fabrics, and wore more tailored clothes, she was asked to represent her company overseas. The reality is that personal impeccability reflects professional success.

An additional concern many women have is how to present themselves professionally if they have gained weight. Several of my clients are middle-aged executives who have added pounds over the years. Each realized that,

3. Understand what flatters your body type, and get a tailor. Clothes that you buy off-the-rack may be too tight or too loose. Either way, showing off too much or looking sloppy is not going to look professional.

One successful executive I know happens to be a tall, full-figured blonde. She spent many years fighting to be taken seriously in the workplace. Proud of her appearance, she didn't understand what was holding her back. Over time, however, she realized that by pulling her

to maintain a leadership position, she would need a different type of wardrobe, along with an updated hairstyle and even new glasses.

Learning to adjust to the many physical changes we experience throughout a business career is important to maintaining a professional image. Making incremental adjustments as we transition through postcollege, childbearing, and menopausal years is essential. Maintaining consistency is the key. Impression management research shows that consistency is an important factor in building credibility. All these tweaks add up to looking like a modern, professional woman.

Being a leader requires skills of negotiation, emotional intelligence, and the sophistication to project a businesslike image. Because a first impression is the front line of our professionalism, it's critical that we get the personal packaging right—specifically, wardrobe fit, color, and quality. If those aren't present, then we won't be taken seriously, and others won't bother looking deeper for content, knowledge, and capability.

While all this may sound unfair, adding the advantage of a professional image will go a long way to breaking down the barriers that hold us back from what we deserve in our careers—success!

hair back and downplaying her figure, she didn't have to fight quite so hard for her work to be respected.

Make an Impression With Your First Impression
Have you ever seen a beautiful painting without a frame? It's attractive, but not nearly as attractive as it could be. A frame can make a painting look larger or smaller, valuable or trivial, and can make the difference between just having something hanging on the wall versus having a work of art carry the room. Although your physical body is the "canvas," and your clothing, accessories, and grooming the "paint," the way you communicate provides that all-important "frame."

In the first thirty seconds, someone you meet for the first time will form an opinion of you. Your impression can be an asset or a hindrance, as it will influence all the information that person receives from you until their opinion changes (which I guarantee will take longer than thirty seconds). Make your first impression work for you. Ask someone for feedback on the kind of first impression you make.

What factors affect a first impression? Think about the times in recent memory in which you've met someone new. What contributed to the impression they made on you? How did the following items affect your impression?

- ◆ **Attire:** The other day, a friend advised an ambitious professional to dress for the job that she wanted. The principle behind this advice is very true. How you are dressed will definitely make an impression. Be sure to know the dress codes of your industry (and company) and the special events you'll be attending (from conferences to company picnics).

  In a 2004 article for which I was interviewed, entitled "What Can We Learn from Donald Trump's 'The Apprentice?'", I advised, "Look and behave like a pro. Some women dressed poorly early in the show. Their foul language and lack of communication skills were disconcerting, to say the least."

  I had thought they looked more like they were dressing for a date than to compete for a $250,000-a-year corporate executive position. As Maureen Costello advises, every time you get dressed, you should ask yourself, "What is the message I'm sending?"

- **Etiquette:** How do you sit in a chair? What do you do with your hands? How do you cross your legs? All of these things are part of your package. How is your etiquette at the table in a restaurant? Do you know how to make small talk, and which fork to use? These things also contribute to the impression people have of you. And, if you don't know a point of etiquette, ask a trusted mentor. Many organizations now offer etiquette training, which, based on what I've seen, many people could use. How do you measure up?

- **Eye Contact:** Look people in the eye. It conveys interest, openness, and connectedness. Look at the other person (not the floor or the ceiling) when shaking hands. Have you ever been in a situation with someone who was constantly looking over your shoulder to see who else was in the room? What was your impression of that person? Remember, eyeball-to-eyeball makes the most impact.

- **Fitness:** Your physical presence also plays an important role in your look. People who exercise regularly radiate a more energetic presence. I am no bodybuilder or marathoner, but I've used a treadmill while watching the news and get up to walk at 6 A.M. to beat the Arizona heat. Ensuring that I exercise regularly helps build my physical strength and stamina. I learned that the edge exercise gives you is to produce more energy than it expends. Be committed and make the time. Thirty minutes per day is all it takes.

- **Voice:** How strong and powerful is your voice? A soft voice makes others have to work too hard to listen, so they tend to tune out. On the other hand, a loud voice can be embarrassing as it allows everyone to hear the conversation. Do you speak too fast or too slow? Do you enunciate your words clearly? Do you have an accent that works against you? Be aware of your tendencies. Many people speed up or lower their voices when they are nervous. Listen to your voice on your voicemails or on your answering machine. What kind of impression does it make? I have always wanted to emulate the authoritative voice of a radio or TV announcer, which is very pleasing to my ear.

- **Handshake:** Think about the last time someone shook your hand: Did it crush your knuckles? Was it a firm and complete grip, or did it provide a very weak grasp of just your fingers? The type of handshake will tell you something about the person (such as their degree of extroversion or introversion). I definitely am affected when someone gives me a "finger shake," or a weak handshake. Do you have a strong handshake in return?

- **Nametags:** Where do you wear a nametag? I've noticed many instances where people introducing themselves at conferences and networking functions wear their nametags inappropriately. Nametags should be worn on your right lapel. The reason? When you shake hands, your eyes generally go to the other person's right to see their nametag, not the left. When I began my career, our nametags had instructions on the back: "Place on your right lapel."

It is vital to present yourself to everyone with a level of confidence and sociability that will get you remembered. Your goal is to build a bond.

How often does the following happen to you? People come up to you and expect you to recognize them. You do, but you can't remember their names. When this happens, shake hands and say your name. This will often remind people to say their own names. If they don't, you can ask politely, "Now what was your name again?"

When you are going around the table introducing yourself during a function, what do you reveal about yourself? This is a marketing opportunity not only to convey information but also to make an impression, such as through offering a memorable or humorous introduction.

Create a thirty second introduction ("commercial") for yourself that captures who you are and how you want to be remembered.

Mentioning what you do and for what company during your introduction can open doors with those you meet. For example, when introducing herself, a woman let me know that she was from Rutgers University. That was great, because I happened to have a friend who teaches there who she also knew, and another person at the same meeting turned out to be a very good friend of my professor friend as well—so we had an instant connection.

If you happen to be at a function such as a conference or large group meeting, sharing who you are and what you do is a free method of advertising. Take the opportunity to make a comment or ask a question in front of the group. Take advantage of question-and-answer sessions. How often do you see someone ask a question and then sit down, leaving people to wonder who they are or why they might have asked that particular question? Get used to introducing yourself (by name and company or division) to the speaker before asking your question. You never know who will be listening in the audience and may want to know who you are as well, either for context for your point of view or to be able to follow up with you.

Interviewing = Selling Yourself to Others

The importance of optimizing your product and package is undeniable when it comes to interviewing for a job. Having interviewed many job candidates over the course of my career, I know that the person who lands the job is not simply the person with the best credentials. Many other things come into play: the caliber of the person, their personal style, their values, their perceived ability to make a contribution (that is, their potential) in my organization, their enthusiasm and desire for the job, to name a few.

Besides focusing on all the qualities that can make a great first impression, job applicants in general must take the time to research the companies with which they are interviewing. This can make a world

A Roundup of Experts on
Creating a Great First Impression

Because different people perceive things differently, I'm happy to share the advice of some leading experts on how to create a great first impression.

From her perspective as a top executive recruiter, Millington McCoy emphasizes the literal importance of the first minute of encountering someone else. "I have learned that in the first thirty seconds you meet someone new, you get a brief glimpse of the real person," she observes. "One of my tests is, can they meet my gaze, or do they melt? If they melt, then I have concerns about that person's ability to relate effectively to senior management. Obviously this doesn't work for everyone. I used this wisdom to train my young son at about age five. He was interested in power, and I told him this secret, and he used it wisely. He was always regarded as poised, confident, and interested in others from a very young age."

Howard Childs, the former photographer for Tina Brown's *Talk* magazine, has shot everyone from Harry Belafonte to Uma Thurman. When asked about first impressions of new people he meets, he comments that "Eye contact is very important, as is how many times the person uses my name." These two items help to establish a general comfort level with another person.

Katherine King, of Leslie Diversity Marketing, observes that a person's handshake is very telling. "In addition, does the person come across as being delighted to meet me? Or do they act uninterested (by looking around the room, for instance, during the conversation)?" she asks. She sees the latter as very rude.

Human resources futurist Anne Hyde also puts a lot of stock in handshakes. "When I meet somebody for the first time, I notice the type of handshake they give me. This action is the first communication that is given by the other person and can say a great deal," she says. "Another communication is how they sit. Do they sit on the edge of the chair with nervousness, or sit back with alert confidence and listen carefully to the questions being asked, waiting until the end of the questioning before answering? In other words, do they listen to what is being asked rather than responding to what they anticipate you are going to be asking?"

Consulting manager Amy Gowder underscores the importance of attire. "While some may consider clothes [to be] superficial, an outfit provides me a lot of information about a person's personality. On a first meeting, I will notice when a person's clothes are very different from the average dress of the crowd:

- *More Formal:* I view them as more reserved or I assume they wish to be viewed as first and foremost a professional.
- *Trendy:* Someone who is dressed with current fashion trends shows signs of energy and enjoys current events. Sometimes new fashion trends are inappropriate in business settings; in this case I would assume this person is new to the business world and below typical maturity or experience.
- *Bright Colors:* If someone wears bright colors as opposed to neutral ones, my first impression is that they are energetic and are not afraid of—or even enjoy—the spotlight.
- *Underdressed:* Finally, someone who is underdressed or dressed much more casually than others gives me an impression of a person who is laid back, prefers informal interactions, or may be involved in a scientific type of job as opposed to business. When someone's dress is drastically more casual, I will assume that they are low energy or perhaps inexperienced in the business world.

A Final Note: Of course, sometimes dress is a factor of timing, such as when someone in a suit may be coming from a more formal meeting and didn't have time to change. However, until I learn those details through interaction, a person's style of dress leads me to conclusions about a person's demeanor and personality."

of difference to someone without much experience. They can gain an edge through their knowledge of the company (how the company makes money, what business it's in, the responsibilities required of the role they're interviewing for, etc.), especially if the ideas they bring to the interview can help the company be more successful.

State your experiences in such a way that the interviewer will be assured that you already have the skills and capabilities to do the work—with a minimal learning curve. Even if you have been out of the work force, quantify and qualify how you have spent your time and have made contributions in other arenas.

For example, several years back an acquaintance of mine, who was not in the traditional work force for quite some time, was appointed to the board of directors of Amtrak. Her ability to successfully portray her career and accomplishments as a volunteer with the Junior League and how her experiences could be translated to serve the board convinced it that she was a perfect fit.

In another instance, a woman went for an interview without being prepared at all. She was an exceptional candidate with great potential, but had not taken the time to understand the company or the type of work she would be expected to do. She was turned down for the job. She not only wasted her time, but the time of the recruiters and others involved in the interview process. Remember, if you aren't willing to do the homework to be rewarded with a position, don't sign up.

To Get the Part, First Master the Role

As I was developing my skills to become a partner, my mentor said to me: "Susan, if you want to be a partner, act like a partner. During conversations regarding your promotion, you want your advocate to be able to demonstrate that you have, in fact, served in the capacity of a partner this past year."

If you are pursuing a promotion, "acting as if" you were promoted is a tool that can greatly augment your product's perceived value. By acting as if you are the perfect person for the position, and having been seen as already working in the position you want, then you may indeed become the ideal candidate.

In order to "act as if" you are in the position, make sure that you know the roles and responsibilities that you need to demonstrate. Keep the following tips in mind:

- Develop an understanding of the requirements of the position, the roles, responsibilities, relationships, expectations, skills and capabilities, etc.
- Identify individuals within the organization to whom you feel comfortable speaking, and recruit them to be on your team to help you achieve the position.
- Develop your product to meet the requirements of the position.
- Ensure that your advocate is aware of your achievements.

Know Your Strengths — and Your Weaknesses

As a product, ensure that you are constantly new and improved. By regularly assessing whether you are the best product on the market, you'll also open yourself to new opportunities to grow and to meet new people.

Getting to know yourself is the first step. For example, when you go in for your annual physical, your doctor will run some tests and evaluate where you are, both compared with your last check-up and compared with your peers (others of your gender and age). In some cases, the early identification of changes or irregularities that escape the naked eye can save your life. In the same vein, it can be just as critical to saving your career to conduct similar tests and self-evaluations that will allow you to find out where you are and what changes you need to make. Learning more about yourself is the preventive medicine that allows you to be proactive about ensuring that your product is up to par.

The process starts with being honest with yourself. Honesty is vital to understanding both your strengths and your weaknesses. Your strengths will likely propel you to achieve the level of success you would like to attain, whereas your weaknesses could prevent you from achieving your potential. So, take the time to get to know yourself: What do you like? What don't you like? What are you good at? When do you tend to fail? What are your other characteristics and preferences? What do others say and think about you?

In most cases, you will need to change yourself by enhancing your skills, building new capabilities, or having new experiences. You will learn this by listening to what others have to say about you and by proactively asking for constructive feedback.

Product Development Opportunities: Become a Feedback Addict

One of the biggest mistakes I initially made in my career was not getting proper feedback. Many people I worked with would simply say, "Susan, you are doing just fine." Not really knowing what they meant, I assumed I was moving ahead quite nicely. Which I was, sort of. Getting specific and timely feedback on how others perceived me would have helped me to know how well I was really doing. There would have been no assumptions necessary.

While quantitative goals are easier against which to measure progress, more qualitative goals require the input of others and are more judgmental. We all have blind spots as we progress in our careers. However, when these weaknesses or "opportunities for improvement" (as they're often referred to in the language of performance reviews) are pointed out, they need to be understood so that they can be addressed. Ask for examples to support and further clarify the feedback you receive.

I can't overemphasize the importance of truly understanding the details so that you can be responsive to feedback. Perception *is* reality. You might disagree with some of the feedback you receive, but the fact is that if others perceive you differently from the way you perceive yourself, *their* perceptions are what *you* need to change.

There are usually plenty of people who will be candid with you, if you ask them to be. Remember that you have to *want* to be helped—or else you just won't be open to benefiting from the guidance that is available.

I remember receiving feedback in a performance review that said I wasn't detail-oriented enough. The first time I heard it, I should have asked for examples and specific ways I could improve. Had I had a clearer idea of the perceived problem, I would have had a better chance of improvement. You shouldn't stop asking questions until you clearly understand the examples and the implications of not making the requested changes. Additionally, you might want to ask the deliverer of the information if he or she would be willing to coach you while you make the improvements.

Giving and Receiving Effective Feedback

Feedback is essential for everyone's growth and development, no matter what your occupation. How else will you know how you are doing, whether as an employee, as a club officer, or as a speaker, for example? We all need to know. And, as my friend Carla Paonessa would say, we need to hear the good, the bad, and the ugly.

Given the importance to you and your team of moving forward most productively, you'd think everyone would know how to give and receive feedback effectively. This is not the case.

Accenture's Brian Fox notes that in an employee satisfaction survey he conducted, personal feedback was one of the lower-scoring items. We all know of people who have not been happy with their feedback. As everyone is expected to do a good job for their companies, many find that their reviews are not timely and tend to be one-way conversations that emphasize the negative over the positive, and what isn't working over what is being accomplished. Fox also studied aspects of effective evaluations, which elicited responses such as the following:

- Feedback begins with a look at roles and responsibilities.
- Simple kudos go a long way, and positive comments help concentrate on success.
- Receiving constructive feedback is having something explained to you rather than having someone correct you.

A large part of what Fox's survey teaches us is that people need to ask for feedback. In addition, evaluators need to make themselves available for more informal feedback opportunities and to provide small "thanks" and suggestions along the way.

In thinking about the evaluations I received over the years at Accenture, I recall that they ranged from "You are doing great" to "Requires improvement," and everything in between. In the early days, men didn't feel comfortable giving an evaluation to a woman and didn't want to give bad news because she might cry. When I didn't get promoted to manager when I thought I should have, I know I cried (and in a fancy restaurant, no less). From then on, I kept a box of tissues ready in my office for whomever wanted to use it.

One of my most effective evaluations didn't come until I'd been with the company for nearly twenty years. The partner told me what I was good at, how I was perceived in the organization, and what I needed to do to improve. He really cared and wanted to help me become more successful. And I was, after that meeting.

Conducting a "Mentoring Conversation"

I would describe an ideal evaluation as "a mentoring conversation." It denotes the right spirit of the meeting in that it should be supportive rather than critical. A mentoring conversation should be conducted in a comfortable environment for everyone. I generally like to have it without a table between us, but others find an evaluation in a restaurant a more relaxing setting.

In preparing for your meeting, you should think about what you would like to cover in the conversation. And before the meeting is over, be sure your points have been covered. For instance, they may include the following:

- Significant accomplishments since your last review
- Areas in which you need to improve and how you might accomplish this
- Ways your mentor (or organization) might specifically help you proceed with your current assignment and your career development

◆ Specific feedback you're looking for and concurrence on your career aspirations and where you think you are in the process

Be sure to include a career development discussion. If you are up for a promotion, talk about what you have to do to get it and a realistic time frame. Everyone's expectations should be aligned. If there are job responsibilities that need to change, ask for help in making that happen.

Although you may not agree with all the feedback, you should prepare yourself to listen to and understand what is said, because every perception of your performance should be addressed and resolved. Don't get defensive. Be ready to have any constructive feedback corrected (or on its way) by your next discussion. The last thing you want is for the same points to come up again. Take notes, and be sure to get a copy of your evaluation so you know the points that have been discussed.

It's important to gain concurrence on your points and those presented to you so you can include the information in your implementation plan for You, Inc. Keep in mind that this evaluation is all about enhancing your product and keeping it current, as well as achieving your vision for You, Inc.

Feedback can be requested or provided at any time. It doesn't necessarily need to happen in a formal meeting—nor should it. You should ask for the feedback you need, whenever it can be useful: after giving a speech, writing a report, running a meeting, participating in a meeting, completing a project, etc. I find that I generally have a "gut" reaction of how I did, but I like to have that feeling confirmed. If I think I have failed, talking to someone is essential, because they may not have the same view. This allows me to think more positively about how I did.

After Your Evaluation

You should feel good about your accomplishments and how you have excelled. On the flip side, you may have a tendency to be very hard on yourself. A mentor of mine often told me that I was too hard on myself, that I was my own worst enemy.

Women especially have a tendency to talk about what we didn't do or what didn't happen, instead of what we accomplished. Men talk about what they achieved; women talk about what they didn't. It is easy to fall prey to patterns of negative thought. Once you start obsessing over what you should have done or should have said or whatever you perceive your failure to have been, you already are wasting valuable mental energy. This is a good time to talk to a friend or mentor about the situation to put it behind you and move on. Learn from it, and let it go.

Evaluations Are Really Self-Evaluations

I remember one discussion in which a partner provided me with feedback written by another partner. I asked, "How could he say that about me? I could say the very same thing about him!" The response was a wise one that has stayed with me: "Susan, don't you know that when you do an evaluation of someone else, or you see something in another person that you like or don't like, it is usually a self-evaluation of your own strengths or shortcomings?" That lesson has stood the test of time. Even today, when I want to provide feedback to someone else, I'll immediately stop to think first, "Do I do this? If so, am I working on improving myself?"

Consider how you evaluate others. In many cases, things you see in *others* are often your *own* strengths or shortcomings. Once you realize this, your evaluations of others can become a good source of information about yourself.

★ ★ ★

Every moment of every day is a marketing opportunity. Your product and packaging are tools to help you get to where you want to be. Working to perfect them—and learning from others how best to market yourself—will be an ongoing process as you navigate your journey.

CHAPTER 6 RECAP

LESSON #16: Your product and package are vitally important to the success of You, Inc.

LESSON #17: Market yourself every hour of every day.

LESSON #18: Know your strengths—and how to compensate for your weaknesses.

ACTION ITEMS:

- Take a snapshot of yourself today. How appropriate is your "look" for your current work environment and that which you aspire to achieve? Give the picture to a trusted colleague, and ask him or her the same question.
- Write a thirty-second commercial for You, Inc.
- Make a list of a few people who wowed you with the first impression they made. What impressed you the most? What can you learn from them?
- Seek out opportunities to improve your communication skills. For example, a local organization like Toastmasters could be a good resource.
- Reading list:
  - *First Impressions: What You Don't Know about How Others See You,* by Ann Demarais, PhD, and Valerie White, PhD
  - *How to Make People Like You in 90 Seconds or Less,* by Nicholas Boothman
  - *Crucial Conversations: Tools for Talking When the Stakes Are High,* by Kerry Patterson et al.
- Request either a formal or informal "mentoring conversation" with your mentor or supervisor.

REFLECT AND RECORD:

- Think of someone you know whom you admire for the way they present themselves to others. Why do you admire that person? What would others say about you?

- When is the last time you felt confident you made a great first impression? Why did you feel that way?
- When you are marketing yourself, what do you tend to do right? What do you need to work on?

-7-

TIME:
USE IT OR LOSE IT

"It is only when we truly know and understand that we have a limited time on earth, and that we have no way of knowing when our time is up, that we will begin to live each day to the fullest; as if it was the only one we had."

—ELIZABETH KÜBLER ROSS

Once You, Inc. is beautifully packaged and its product is focused and prepared, you will be ready to run the day-to-day tasks of achieving your goal. If the operational aspects of You, Inc. are managed efficiently, your climb to the top will be swift and steady. What's more, your life will achieve balance.

The key to running You, Inc. will be managing your resources. Resources are scarce assets—whether time, people, or capital—so you'll want to make the most of those at your disposal. Careful planning of how you utilize them is essential.

Are You Spending—or Investing—Your Time?

As CEO, an important thought about running You, Inc. should be "How can I manage my time most efficiently?" Time is our most valuable resource. It is irreplaceable. You'll never have today's twenty-four hours to use again—how will you use them?

Everyone has the same number of hours in a day, from a high school senior to the president of the United States. Our time is all about how we choose to use it. Do you keep track of how you use your time? Are you reaping as much benefit as possible from your choices?

Look at what is on your "to do" list. Do you have enough time to do the things *you* want to do? How can you best prioritize? I will venture to guess that you have too much on your plate and that you are spending at least some of your time on the wrong things. I know that I always have too much going on because there is so much I want to do. I'll occasionally hear the voice of my mentor in my head reminding me, "Susan, you need to learn to focus."

When I review my list of things to do, there are always a few things that have been there a long time. Why haven't I been able to get them done? Sometimes it's a matter of not having a fixed deadline. Other times, I seem to just procrastinate about certain items, especially when something more interesting captures my attention. Still other times, the items should not have been there in the first place, because they're simply not that important to me.

An example of the latter is my longtime "to do" of finding time to play golf. Arizona, where I live part of the year, is the Shangri-la of winter golf, and everyone always says I should get out on the course. Well, I finally decided that wasn't going to happen, so I asked myself why I was always saying it was something I wanted to do? Now, that item is officially gone—no longer in my mind and no longer taking up space on my mental "to do" list.

Know Your "A-List" — and Always Keep Your Vision in Focus

Because time is arguably your most precious asset, one of the most important steps you can take to evaluate how you are progressing is to analyze how you're spending it and determine whether it's in sync with your priorities.

Your daily schedule indicates where you spend your time. Your A-list consists of the items you need to do to accomplish your goal. How does your actual daily schedule compare to your A-list, which is where you should invest your time? You get to decide anew every morning where your next twenty-four hours are going to be spent. Are you happy with the return you are getting from the places in which you invest your time?

Make clear distinctions about your time. Are you receiving value for it? Is anyone receiving value? If not, are you wasting your time? If something is a drag on your energy yet needs to get done, then maybe someone else can do it who might actually find the experience valuable, even exciting.

The way to make sure your vision becomes reality is to keep focused on the big picture and not let others' goals distract you. Your goal should always drive what you do. Your A-list of activities is designed to help you get to where you want to be. Treat these things as sacred, and let their positive momentum drive how you allocate your time.

As an example, I compared some of the ways I spent my time to my A-list. As a member of Accenture's Capital Committee, I used to attend four-hour meetings every two weeks. I wasn't contributing to the meetings, and the information under discussion was not essential to know to do my job. Therefore, I got out of my commitment to attend the meetings and instead simply read the minutes after each meeting.

That freed up eight additional hours in my schedule every month, during which I was able to focus on what was most important to me and my job. Eight hours doesn't sound like much until it's handed to you like a gift to spend on whatever you choose. We never have enough time, so be sure you are investing your time where you will receive the greatest return.

In a similar vein, at a lunch event with iVillage cofounder Candice Carpenter in New York City, I met a top woman executive with AT&T who explained to me why she'd opted not to serve on several boards. "I added up the number of hours I not only put in at board meetings but also, in preparing for them and traveling to them, and decided that it wasn't worth it," she told me. "They weren't contributing to my vision—and I decided I needed more time for my business and me. I resigned and let them find someone who was really excited about the board positions."

Certainly, for those of you coming up in your organization, you can gain knowledge and networking opportunities from being on committees and attending meetings. Your A-list should include such opportunities for growth. So, what can you afford to give up to better prioritize your time? Gaining time for yourself can be as simple as reading the paper on the train instead of at your desk in the morning. Get up an hour earlier. Shop online instead of trekking to the mall. You may want to spend a week really noting how you spend your time and thinking of how to better invest it.

Schedule—and Live—Your Priorities

Studies have shown that the most successful people are those whose lives are "in balance" and who enjoy what they do. Work is so much easier when you enjoy your life. While all jobs have elements of drudgery, it's important to think about the "fun factor"—and to evaluate it from time to time and consider what might need to change to bring more joy into your work and your life.

As previously mentioned, the critical first step is to put your A-list commitments on your calendar as soon as possible. Then, as they come up, let others on your team know if there is a conflict with an A-item and see whether there is a way to work it out.

Keep in mind that it's important for you to know and communicate your priorities and commitments. For example, imagine being asked to help out with an important project over the weekend. You had long-standing plans to attend an event that was important to you. If something is important to you, take responsibility to inform your supervisor of the conflict and provide a recommendation so that together you might be able to find a win-win solution. She is not a mind reader, yet I know of so many people who, instead of communicating openly and honestly, end up resenting their bosses for not respecting their need for a balanced life.

My A-list includes things that are focused on women and girls, activities that help me network strategically, opportunities that lead to selling my book, thinking time, mentoring time, institute initiatives, journaling time, exercise time, and time for myself. The list has shifted as my priorities have changed over time, and I consciously make adjustments as the need arises.

Although I often traveled internationally during my career, I always liked to be in Tucson on the weekends. It was on my A-list. To accomplish this, I put the Arizona trips on my calendar as far in advance as possible. And while I knew that I would not make it to Tucson every weekend, it became *my* decision to remove the trip from my calendar.

In most cases, I have found that if I want to do something badly enough, I can usually figure out a way to make it happen. By remaining as true as possible to what is most important to you, you will operate from a position of control with complete understanding and acceptance of the decisions. This is just another way of making things happen *for* you, instead of letting them happen *to* you.

Always Ask: "What's In It for Me?"

While you're on your way to achieving your big goal, it may help to prioritize your use of time if you ask yourself, "What's in it for me?" (My acronym for this is WIIFM, pronounced WIFF-em.) In other words, how can *you* benefit, such as improving your product, while you are contributing to a project? This approach will provide you with an opportunity to proactively enhance your product. There is always something you can do better or differently to increase your learning, and it's up to you to determine what that is.

You can decide what to spend time on by looking at each task from a You, Inc. perspective. For example, at the beginning of every new project, you should ask yourself, "How am I going to use this as an opportunity to improve my product?" There are lots of ways for you to benefit from a project, even—or especially—one similar to another you've already completed. For example, figure out a way to do it differently to develop new skills or become more efficient.

There will be times when non–A-list items will put demands on your time. For example, when your superior asks that you stop what you are working on to do her a favor, you can't refuse, although you may resent the interruption. Instead of begrudgingly doing what she requests, do it while thinking about You, Inc. Think, "How can I get something for me (a new skill, or a new relationship) while I am doing this work?" You may figure out a way that the request supports your A-list after all.

If you're hard pressed to find value in the majority of your assignments (that is, they are not getting you to where you want to be), you might consult with your mentors: would they say you have "topped out" in your current position? What steps would they recommend you take to advance in your career?

Create New, Productive Habits

Bad habits tend to be easy to make and hard to break. If you can train yourself to develop new and better habits, you can literally re-create your life. What are your current habits, those often unconscious patterns of behavior? How can you eliminate the habits that no longer serve you (for example, eating junk food, smoking, always running late) and instill new ones? What habits would serve you better (such as eating better, exercising daily, always being on time)?

Determining where you presently spend your time and where you want to spend your time are important exercises—in fact, they are two of the most important you'll ever use. Once you figure out how you want to spend your time, commit to investing it in making things happen rather than letting others spend it for you. You should think about it every single day. Establishing new, productive habits as a part of your routine will help ensure that your time is spent on A-list items.

The following are some habits you may want to acquire:

- Never start a project with a blank sheet of paper. When you have a new assignment, find out who has had a similar task, and learn from their experience. If it's a report to be written, look at a similar type of report that has been written for this person. I can assure you it will save you a lot of time. Also, when you tackle an assignment similar to one you have done before, make your first step figuring out how to take advantage of being further up the learning curve to do it faster and better.

- Learn how to delegate. I still need to work on the level of detail I choose to get involved with. The year I started my institute, I wanted to be a part of all of the details behind my institute's inaugural Women's Leadership Development Conference held at the University of Arizona. As of the second year, it is student led, and I work only on a few strategic items, such as determining the agenda and inviting the speakers. The rest is up to the committee. Delegation is a growth opportunity for others. Show them the ropes, and then let them run with it.

- Additionally, I "outsource" activities I really don't want or like to do, such as housework. You should too. Consider the time you will save by outsourcing. It will provide you with more time to use on your A-list activities.

- Prioritize and get things done. I recently drew a picture of everything that I (as CEO of Me, Inc.) was involved in or wanted to be involved in. After doing so, I realized that there was not enough time in the day, or days in the year, for me to do all of what was in the picture.

I recalled my thoughts on the importance of focus as I viewed the picture I had created. Try this exercise: draw a picture of everything that you, the CEO of You, Inc., are or want to be involved in, and see whether your own results might be improved by focusing your attention.

- Be deadline driven. We generally get tasks done when they are due or when they become pressingly urgent. Create self-imposed deadlines for your tasks. Also, define the amount of time you are going to invest in a given task. How much time is it worth? Stick to the estimate if possible.

- Determine when it is time to stop. There is a point when enough is enough, and spending more time on the task won't increase the value of the product by much. Control the task too, and don't let the scope expand. Learn to stop at just the right point. Make a point of referring back to your original time estimate so that you can improve in your ability to estimate how long a project or task will take. This will benefit your project management skills in the long-term.

- Don't push yourself to frustration. Be aware of what happens to your work if you become upset. In either case, give yourself a cooling-off period. A friend shared this example: "When I get an upsetting e-mail that turns my stomach, I invoke a '24-hour rule.' That is, I cool off before I respond, because if I respond immediately, I will inevitably create more problems through what I might say and then spend more time in the long run resolving the situation."

- Touch a piece of paper once. Don't waste time by touching the same piece of paper, mail, or e-mail twice. Stephanie Winston writes in her bestselling book, *Getting Organized,* about her now-famous TRAF system:
  - *T* is for *Toss:* If the information or document is something that can go in the trash, put it there.
  - *R* is for *Refer:* If the best action is to refer the problem or issue to someone else, do it!

- - *A* is for *Action:* Take action on the item, and get it off your desk or list.
  - *F* is for *File:* Once you're done, file the document only if you'll *really* need it later.
- ◆ Use e-mail efficiently. How much time do you spend reading e-mail you don't need to read? How much time do you spend responding to e-mail? Are your e-mails too long or too short? Are you sending information to people who don't need to get it? You may be wasting your time and the reader's time. Be sure you use the TRAF system when dealing with e-mail.

Juggling Multiple Objectives

Any well-rounded person may have a multitude of balls in the air at any given time. Each goal will have a different motivation and will require a different level of commitment and time—and prioritization. To make sure you know where each goal stands in relation to your others, sum each up with a tagline that will keep you focused and on track.

Some objectives may suffer while you focus on others, but you should strive to achieve the balance necessary for them to all come to fruition. One way to overcome any ambivalence (there's that *A*-word again!) that might be getting in the way of taking action toward achieving your goals is to remind yourself of all the reasons you wanted to achieve them in the first place. Think about giving your key projects a tagline that will help motivate you. Let's face it: we all need to be sold sometimes! And it works. For example, when you put on your sneakers to run out the door, you could think of it as your "Get Fit" campaign.

So if your plan is to find a way to "get out of my warm bed earlier to go outside in the cold and work out," that's just not going to have the same motivating power as using the tagline "Lose 5 (pounds) in 5 (weeks)." You might develop a bold title for your plan to get promoted: "Conquest for the Corner Office."

What will the taglines be for your overall mission, and for each of the divisions of You, Inc. (that is, for each of your major goals)? Consider the following examples:

- Your overall mission: "Being the Best Me I Can Be"
- Your career: "Promote Myself into a Promotion"
- Your family and friends: "Reach Out and Touch Someone I Love"
- Your health and well-being: "Lose Five in Five"
- Your environment: "Say It to Myself with Flowers"
- Your financial security: "What I Invest Now, I Won't Have to Earn Later"
- Your enjoyment of life: "Life Is Either a Daring Adventure or Nothing"

Often, your goals will intersect—which is why it's important to test them for compatibility. Together, your action plans should comprise a synergistic masterpiece that is a blueprint for creating the *you* that you wish to become.

Your Life as a Series of Decisions (When to Say Yes and When to Say No)

The decisions you make dictate how the precious resource of your time is spent. Every day, you make decisions that will affect your future, your implementation plan (moving you toward your goal), or your vision. Certain decisions will open up new opportunities to you, while closing off other paths. For example, if you are intent on a career in business and would like to attend graduate school in a field that will help you advance in your career, you might consider earning a degree in business, international relations, or law. But opting for a business degree over a law degree will preclude your becoming a lawyer, while opting for a law degree over an MBA won't preclude your becoming a businessperson.

In life, there are no such things as perfect choices—only smart choices. So, make sure your decisions are well-informed and well thought-out.

Along the same line, it's an important life skill to learn when to say yes and when to say no. When you say yes, remember that you are making a commitment. If you don't have time, say so. If you don't have time but want to do it, ask for the help you need to reprioritize your responsibilities. Saying yes and not delivering is worse than saying no. Others remember the result much longer.

In the instance when the assignment you're asked to take on is something that you may not have done before, your natural tendency may be to say no. Is this a "smart" decision? Why are you tempted to say no? Is it because you truly don't have the skills, or is it because you don't have the confidence in yourself to do the work? The person asking you obviously thought you could do it. Say no if you truly are not the right person for the job. Otherwise, say yes. This is a good way to build your confidence. This golden rule was taught to me by a mentor after I once refused an opportunity I should have accepted.

When I was working in Accenture's Chicago office, I turned down an opportunity to work in São Paulo, Brazil. Although I was flattered that the partner there had considered me for the project, it didn't feel right to me. It was only in retrospect during a conversation with my mentor that the reason I said no became clear. I realized that it wasn't that I lacked the skills to handle the assignment; I lacked the confidence in myself.

I learned an important lesson: always evaluate the reason for saying no to an opportunity before it slips away. Although we may know we can accomplish anything we set our minds to, sometimes our lack of confidence gets in our way. We can remind ourselves of this by reviewing examples of times when this has been proven to be true, or by talking with mentors who have confidence in us and can remind us.

Before saying no, consider the likely outcome if you say yes instead, and land an opportunity to build new confidence and skills.

★ ★ ★

Time is your most valuable asset. It is available to use as you see fit, so why not use each and every moment you can toward achieving your vision? There are smart ways to invest your time instead of spending it frivolously. (Not that you shouldn't include 'have fun' on your A-list!) But, each item on your A-list should support your vision of a balanced and fruitful life—however you have envisioned it.

CHAPTER 7 RECAP

LESSON #19: Use your A-list to keep you focused.
LESSON #20: Invest your time instead of spending it.
LESSON #21: There are no perfect choices—just smart ones.
LESSON #22: Know when to say yes and when to say no.

ACTION ITEMS:

◆ List the items on your A-list. Are they on your schedule? Are the tasks in which you are involved supporting your A-list? If not, why are you doing them?

◆ Create taglines for the activities that will support you in achieving your vision and in turn support your A-list.

◆ Make a list of the habits you would like to eliminate. Make another list of positive habits you would like to acquire. Document how you will go about making these improvements.

REFLECT AND RECORD:

◆ Can you think of a time when you should have said yes to an opportunity but did not have the confidence to take on the challenge? When did you say no and why? How did that make you feel?

◆ What parts of your life can you streamline (or eliminate) to gain more time to focus on your A-list?

-*8*-

YOU ARE
THE CONNECTIONS
YOU WEAVE

"If you have knowledge, let others light their candles in it."

—MARGARET FULLER

A s you continue to navigate your journey, you'll find nothing as complex as managing your interactions with the people with whom you come into contact. That said, these people at your office, club, church, conferences, or other venues are essential resources to help you achieve your goal.

Using people as a resource is certainly not as cold and heartless as it sounds. Each interaction we have is a mutual sharing of interest or information that can potentially help either party. Interaction is not just a one way street. Connecting to people with grace and generosity is the surest way to get them on your side. Even in today's competitive world, playing fair and helping out when needed never fails. After all, you belong to a community of people who rely on each other to succeed.

"Net"working

At the time of this writing, there are approximately six billion people in the world. What if you could focus the power of some of them to help you achieve your goal? Better yet, what if you could focus the power of *many* of them to help you achieve it?

In fact, you can. The secret is focusing on the power of effective networking, which will help you build the brand of You, Inc.

I once worked on a strategic networking project to better understand the various types of networks that exist. The first type of network consists of people who only know each other and who are unknown to people outside their group. Some might say they have all of their eggs in one basket. The career progress of these individuals was found to be very limited. No one outside their group knew them or what they did.

The second type of network, and the most beneficial to one's career, was found to be a strategic network. A strategic network is one in which (1) you know a group of people, (2) each of them knows another group of people, and (3) each person or group offers you the means to meet more people that you want to know and who should know you.

The reason this is referred to as "strategic" is that you can proactively identify who you want to get to know (for example, key people in your industry) based on your strategy for You, Inc., and then strategically figure out how you can meet them through the people you know.

Experienced networkers know that their networks invariably include links to other networks. I have many smaller networks that comprise my broader strategic network: my Accenture network, my Purdue network, my network of women's groups, my Tucson and Oregon networks, my education network, my philanthropy network, my food and wine enthusiast network, and so on. My life is a series of interwoven networks that can achieve powerful results for me and for those I know.

There are three different stages of networking:

Stage I: Turning strangers into acquaintances

Stage II: Turning acquaintances into useful allies

Stage III: Recruiting members of your team who will help you succeed

Using the analogy of a net is useful in understanding each stage. For the first stage, for example, picture a net being cast into the sea. A coarse net will catch fewer fish (and only the largest ones), while a fine net will catch more fish (both large and small ones). What kinds of fish will *your* net catch? In other words, whom would it be most useful for you to meet, get to know, and have as part of your network—and where and how can you best "catch" them? To achieve your goal, a step in your plan needs to be defining the networks of which you want or need to be a part.

One idea is to turn to places where you're likely to meet new people who have something in common with you or something you're seeking, such as alumni organizations, churches, and professional associations. But it's also a matter of being open to those people you meet through serendipity—from your neighbors to your yoga teacher. And it's a matter of getting to know them and then, moving into the second stage, connecting to them—just as a knot connects two ropes in a net. Through the second stage, you'll learn more about which connections may be helpful to you and develop a hierarchy of the people you turn to most often. Why? Because you like them, trust them, or can count on them to deliver results. Hopefully, it's a matter of all three, as each of these qualities should characterize each of the members of the team you recruit in stage three.

It's Not What You Know—It's Who You Know

I believe I was born a networker. Girl Scouts and the 4-H Club were just a warm-up for my professional life. However, the first professional networking organization that I remember joining officially was the American Society of Women Accountants (ASWA). My original purpose in becoming a member of the ASWA was to learn more about the accounting field. Because I was working for an accounting firm, I thought I should know what the business was all about. Little did I know that the organization would allow me to find my first woman mentor, become a mentor to other women who were the first women in their organizations, get comfortable speaking about my technology consulting experiences, and develop leadership skills and experiences as a national officer and a member of the national board. It also recently provided me the opportunity to speak at their annual meeting of over three hundred women.

The three stages of successful networking address why networks are so essential, how to develop a strategic network, and how you can get the most out of it.

Stage One: Turning Strangers Into Acquaintances ("Creating Your Network")

To build a great network, you need a great talent pool from which to draw. This starts with building and maintaining your network from day one of your career. Everyone has, or can have, their own "World Wide Web" to draw on for information and contacts.

Although the term *web* has become synonymous with the Internet, your web can be thought of as a segment of your network that shares certain things in common. These common values or interests or goals provide the "stickiness" that makes a network work. It helps you to attract people and opportunities that will help you reach your goals and your potential, and vice versa.

For instance, if you are a small business owner and want to join a network, I would suggest NAWBO (National Association of Women

Business Owners), where you can learn from other women business owners, find a mentor or two, market your company and perhaps find new clients and build your network of women. Or, if you are in the consumer products or retail industry, I might suggest the Network of Executive Women.

Women's networks are still very important to assist you in developing your career. They are "safe" environments in which to meet other women and talk about issues and problems that you would never discuss with a mixed gender group. You might even find mentors and people for your "network." These associations will also provide you lots of options to develop leadership skills, including speaking opportunities.

What's the difference between being a part of networks and networking? Essentially, you join the former so that you can do the latter. Remember that joining is often only a matter of paying the initiation and membership fees. However, it requires active involvement—such as attending meetings and assuming leadership roles—to reap the potential benefits.

Creating your network must evolve from a *reactive* into a *proactive* pursuit if you want to be successful. Don't wait for your network to come to you. Put yourself in positions where you can meet people who can help you realize your vision. Be prepared: know who you want to meet, research their backgrounds (google them to discover causes or organizations that are important to them, such as industry organizations), and have your business cards ready.

If you are considering joining a networking organization, determine in advance what your networking goals are before you commit the important resources of your time and money. Figure out where you want to make the investment and why, based on the kinds of people you want to meet. The reason may be for business development, to find a mentor, or to support the community. After all, a busy CEO like you doesn't have time to waste.

Alumni organizations are a logical place to turn, as you'll be meeting people who already have something in common with you. Professional organizations will help you meet others within your field. You're likely to meet a much broader range of people through community or church organizations, and some of these connections may be useful or satisfying in yet other ways. Diversification is important.

There are three primary kinds of networking organizations: ones where you (1) can learn from others, (2) can advise others, and (3) are among your peers. ASWA was in the first category for me, as I was primarily on the "receiving" end, learning from many different role models. Later in my career, I spent more time on the advising end. The Committee of 200, an invitation-only professional organization of preeminent women entrepreneurs and corporate leaders, is a network of peers, so we discuss things in which we are all interested in and both give and receive advice. Each kind of organization is very important, especially at different stages of your career.

If you can't find a network to meet your needs, consider starting your own. I organized the Professional Women's Association (PWA) of Chicago in the 1970s. It was an organization for women in all types of businesses who were interested in meeting each other to gain knowledge and network, and to also be committed to participate in an annual philanthropic event. Ideally, you'll come up with a niche that's not yet been identified or served by another network. Then, in this age of the Internet, it's simple: combine email lists with like-minded networkers and reserve a restaurant on a weeknight to kick things off. This can be a tremendous way to meet people and can turn you into a leader overnight. It is interesting to note that several women from PWA are still very good friends and are in my network of great women.

Tom Hines of Northern Trust Bank shared with me one of his favorite books on networking: *Dig Your Well before You're Thirsty* by Harvey Mackay. Mackay reports that the biggest mistake people make is to wait until they need help to establish a network. Tom himself stays in close communication with industry peers and subordinates, which assists him in keeping a full pipeline of potential hires—and keeps him in touch with what his competition is doing.

Don't forget that it doesn't take a formal networking setting to meet useful contacts. Learn to network as a way of life, making it a point to get to know people you might meet by chance.

Here are some ideas that can help you become a smart networker:

- Make a compelling first impression (for example, through your attire, body language, eye contact, handshake). Use your commercial (a description of who you are and what you do that's so compelling that the person to whom you are talking will want to spend time with you) when introducing yourself to others. This is especially important when meeting people with whom you might otherwise find yourself tongue-tied.

- Use the back of the business cards of people you meet to make notes that will help you remember them, as well as any promised follow-up. Be sure to keep in touch. Be confident, empathetic, appreciative, tenacious, and caring, and become a resource for others. You'll be surprised at how quickly your network grows.

- Make it a point to mention your vision and your mission when meeting someone new. Remind people of it regularly by including a descriptive e-mail signature at the bottom of your messages. Or, use holiday greetings as an opportunity to include an "annual report" that recaps your year and summarizes what's on the horizon.

- Bring people from your networks together for a casual meal at a restaurant or even at home serving a favorite recipe, when the only commonality is that all the guests know you. It is a way of cross-pollinating your networks—plus everyone enjoys getting to add a few new people to their networks!

Stage Two: Turning Acquaintances Into Useful Allies ("Working Your Network")

"If you need a reference in Kuwait, have them get in touch with me."
—GENERAL H. NORMAN SCHWARZKOPF,
AFTER RETURNING FROM DESERT STORM, TO SUSAN BUTLER

Several years ago, I was fortunate enough to make the acquaintance of General Schwarzkopf, best known for his services as commander-in-chief, United States Central Command, and commander of operations of the Desert Storm campaign in December 1991. I would have been flattered just to meet him as a social contact. As it turns out, we struck an alliance based on our mutual interests.

At the time I met him, he was visiting one of his retired Army friends in New York. And later, over coffee in the Pentagon, we discussed issues with which we were both dealing. I was amazed one day when he used the phrase "it's lonely at the top." After the war, I met up with him again when he was speaking at Southern Methodist University in Dallas. When we

A Roundup of Experts on Power Networking

The women below work in a variety of different fields, yet all agree that networking is essential for creating the bonds that make your business—and your life—work.

- ◆ Purdue University development director **Lora Adams**: "As busy as we all are, many women find that working in the community as a volunteer is both rewarding and pleasurable. I have found my volunteer experiences also to be a great way to build a network. Unlike networking within your field, networking through volunteer activities pulls together a unique and very diverse group of individuals. The net that binds this sort of group is generally loosely woven, but the common thread is strong enough to build a solid foundation for the network. Through my volunteer networks, I have helped friends and students find jobs, sought financial/mortgage advice, and even secured a reliable dog-sitter!"

- ◆ Nonprofit consultant **Florence Andre**: "Networking has been my main method of obtaining clients over the years as a consultant. I have never advertised or promoted myself in a formal way. Especially in the nonprofit sector, it is not always what you know as much as who you know that will get your foot in the door of a major foundation or corporate giving office."

shook hands, I mentioned my name (just in case he couldn't remember it). "I know who you are," he said, smiling. He was interested in what I was doing, and I told him I was going to Kuwait to potentially do work with their Department of Defense. His parting words to me were, "If you need a reference in Kuwait, have them get in touch with me."

There is an important difference between maintaining a Rolodex and working your network. Although everyone has a Rolodex, which is just a catalog of names, it takes strategy and skill to develop and hone a network of the people on whom can depend. The science of alliances—

- Journalist **Christy Bulkeley** (my cousin) says that she used networks to connect with people who could offer support, help work out ideas, or who had fascinating jobs. She also reflected that we learned this from our fathers who were active in service clubs (such as Rotary) and used them in a similar way.
- Wall Street professional **Katherine Davisson** notes, "Informal networks have been important to me over the years, in terms of seeking advice and serving as a sounding board when I've been faced with important decisions and/or challenges."
- Important aspects of how to build your network came from Harvard Business School Network of Women Alumnae chair **Karen Page**: "Always put your best foot forward. Be respected, and then be liked. A close friend referred a job-seeking colleague to me who spoke of her current job so disparagingly that I didn't feel comfortable referring her in turn to my contacts. A referral depends on someone else's willingness to say, 'OK—you can use my brand.' Be sure to earn the right first. Then, practice basic etiquette. Say, 'please,' 'thank you,' and 'you're welcome.' As you were taught long ago, they really are magic words."

that is, harnessing the power of creating a broad strategic network so your eggs aren't all in one basket in case that basket collapses—and the strategic use of those relationships are key.

The first step in turning acquaintances into useful allies is to get to know selected people from your various networks, such as by inviting them to share a meal or coffee. You want to listen to and remember details about their interests and preferences so that you can become a more useful resource for them. Likewise, you want to make sure that they get to know you, your capabilities, and your aspirations so that they can in turn become more useful resources to you.

Make it a point to keep in touch with members of your network by adding value at every opportunity, such as by forwarding them articles of interest you run across in your reading, inviting them to events (such as to hear prominent speakers) they're likely to enjoy, and referring them to other people they might want to meet. The last creates new interconnections in your network, which makes it even more dynamic and enhances your reputation as a power networker.

How do you make sure you use, but don't abuse, your network? It's important to make sure that any requests you make of people in your network are specific and clear. In addition, especially if it's a big request, it can help to mention WIIFT ("What's In It for Them," in terms of exposure, compensation, connections, goodwill, etc.) and to ensure there is a WIIFT—or to offer a comparable favor, or to take them out to lunch or dinner as a thank-you.

Stage Three: Recruiting Members of Your Team Who Will Help You Achieve Your Aspirations

Out of these networking connections—or alliances—may emerge some natural candidates for your board of directors. They will show themselves by either expressing a special interest in you and your goals or having some specific skill or expertise that you need on your team.

As in all relationships, networking alliances are developed through a mutual interest or connection. The people who will join your team will be more than networking contacts. They will show themselves to be invested in you and your future in some way.

Is Your Energy More Like a Laser Beam or a Dim Bulb?

Be around people who will give you energy, excite you, teach you, and who will expand your horizons. Surround yourself with those who believe in you and will help you achieve your goal.

Because there were so few professional women with whom to connect in the early days of my career, I especially appreciate the energy I receive from being around other women executives in forums such as the Professional Women's Association, AWSA, the *Fortune* Summit, and the annual conferences of the Committee of 200. I find that being around other women who make things happen and who collectively feel like they can conquer the world to be upbeat and exciting.

I'm also energized by being around a broad, eclectic group of people in different fields, and I have learned to share this experience with others by hosting luncheons or other events. Over the years, I've gotten into the habit of giving parties at holiday time when I can mingle friends and acquaintances from every part of my life. Some of them have commented to me with amazement, "Susan, this was a great party—and what a diverse group of friends you have. The only thing we have in common is *you!*"

Office Politics

Amazingly, you may find you spend more time with the people with whom you work than your own close friends and family. For this reason, it's essential you keep in mind several tips for getting along and getting ahead. Whether you work for a large corporation, a small business, or even for yourself, you will come into contact with people in a business setting where—often—the rules of the game go unsaid.

Office relationships tend to be about power—either you are learning from those who hold the power or you are discovering how to use your own power to be a leader to those in your organization. Get comfortable with power.

What does power mean to you? To me, it's about understanding who you are, what you know, what you can accomplish, and how to accomplish it. Invariably, the last aspect involves leveraging the efforts of other people to make things happen.

Too many women tend to be uncomfortable with power. We don't "strut our stuff." Or when we do, we sometimes fear that we come across as bragging or being too aggressive. We need to think about what it means to be powerful. We also need to learn, once we are in positions of power, how to use it without abusing it.

Years ago a friend of mine was promoted to partner in his organization, and I saw the power really go to his head. Virtually overnight, he didn't have time for the "little people" like me anymore. His inflated ego made such an impression on me that I made sure I didn't act likewise once I was promoted. People with power need to work with others to accomplish a goal or complete a project—but in such a way that others will *want* to do it and be on their teams.

Learning to Lead

No matter where you are—in business, school, church, or your home—virtually everything requires a team effort. So, how do you get the most out of a group of people? If you are the leader, turn them into a synergistic team. If you are a part of the team, be on the lookout for leaders who will empower and support you.

Leading a team starts with defining the "North Star," or the outcomes to be achieved by the team, along with the resources (such as time and money) necessary for the team's success. The team must be an integral part of defining the outcomes. The leader is not a manager but someone who helps foster creativity, risk taking, thinking out of the box, and so on. Leaders should also be focused on enhancing the skills and responsibilities of the team members.

Select team members on the basis of their passion for the North Star, and invite these people to "get on the train." (If there are team members who aren't buying into the vision or pulling their weight, they should be invited to "get off the train.") Don't forget to ensure that everyone shares in the success of the team!

Employees told me that they found me to be an empowering leader instead of a command-and-control manager. This, I think, is the secret to inspiring others. What did I do that was different? I believe it boils down to five things:

- Provide a team environment and a clear goal to be met.
- Delegate the work that needs to be done.
- Provide the team members with direction and assistance as necessary to complete their work successfully (without micro-managing).
- Be available to provide timely advice and counseling.
- Provide people with opportunities to develop and advance their careers.

It's important to have a "we" attitude, as opposed to a "me and you" attitude. The best results occur when leaders pay attention to their team members: the work gets done, and people make the leaders look good. The best leaders will make their team members look good as well.

I've found that once you pull together the very best people available and point them in the right direction, as long as you take care of them, they will take care of you.

The Most Important Ingredient: Pay Attention to People

Through assignment after assignment, one principle stood out from all others as the key to success in the process of managing change: because *people* make change happen, any desired change *must* take people into account. Investing in people is one of the most valuable commitments you'll ever make.

In addition to delivering the bottom line, leaders must focus on their people and help them become more effective in their jobs. The return-on-investment (ROI) on capital, for instance, is much easier to measure than the return on human assets—but the latter has the single greatest impact on a business.

Getting the most out of people is one of the best ways to improve your performance today. It is one of the biggest areas of leverage you have to affect your success. Paying attention to people on your project team will pay you huge rewards, to them and to you. Treat them as you would want to be treated yourself. It may sound clichéd, but it is an important lesson, and one that most would admit spurred them on to their best performances.

When I was managing partner of Accenture's Philadelphia office, I made time to check in and talk to everyone in the office, not just my direct reports. This led to a much more tightly knit group and made it clear that I was accessible if they ever needed me. I even encouraged them to call me when they encountered problems.

By doing my "walk-arounds," I picked up a lot of information I wouldn't have learned otherwise. One woman in the office, who returned from maternity leave a few months after I had assumed my position as office managing partner, noted the effect of my actions: "Before I left, people were just doing their jobs," she told me. "But now, people are really on my team, and they're working more closely to deliver value on my client projects."

To pay attention, listen, or say "thank you" to people costs nothing.

Develop Resilience

> *"Resilience: A. the ability to bounce back into shape or position.
> B. the ability to recover strength and good spirits quickly."*
>
> —SUSAN BULKELEY BUTLER

My thoughts on teamwork notwithstanding, interacting with people at the office is not always a bed of roses. For this reason, one of the most vital skills that will help you manage your professional relationships is resilience.

In addressing Accenture's Women's Leadership Forum, former U.S. Secretary of State Madeleine Albright summed up one of the most important lessons of her career, which is relevant to the subject of resilience: "Don't get mad. Disagree, make your points, be confrontational—but don't get mad. When a woman gets mad, a man's response will always be to say that you are just being emotional and to dismiss you."

Failure is a constant in the lives of those who dare to take risks in pursuing their goals. And resilience in the face of disappointment at work is one of the toughest lessons you will learn. The trick is to minimize the chance of failure by following a well thought-out course of action—and to deal well with failure when it actually arrives. Failure can be an opportunity to learn and grow and, as Thomas Edison pointed out, to figure out one more way *not* to do things next time.

It's important to catch mistakes during the planning stage, and to avoid making the same errors again and again. My friend, Bill Boynton, a University of Arizona planetary science professor whose capital-intensive exploits into outer space haven't always yielded the data hoped for, has frequently been known to say, "Education can be expensive—and it tends to teach lessons that you never forget."

★ ★ ★

Life is all about communication. You've thought about your product and your packaging, the whole purpose of which is to best present yourself to people. They are your lifeline to success. It is therefore worth creating the strategic relationships necessary for you to achieve your goals. Once these relationships are in place, it is your job to maintain productive communication and alliances by treating people how you would like to be treated.

A Roundup of Experts on the Topic of Teamwork

I convened a virtual roundtable with a few experts I thought could contribute important insights on the topic of teamwork because I've seen each of them use it to achieve important outcomes.

My Sydney-based friend **Robyn Brown**, who had worked with us on the SAP Power Team at Accenture, shared her thoughts on the essential ingredients of teamwork:

- Leadership is essential. There must be a clear understanding of the team's goals and objectives (such as, Where are we going?), the "rules of the road," timelines, acceptable behaviors, and consequences. The leader should have the wisdom and sound experience to provide good judgment and direction, to anticipate and remove any roadblocks to progress, and to not "do" the work for the team. It is important for team members to take away "lessons learned," and the leader must acknowledge both successes and failures in a positive way.
- Respect for the individual is also an important ingredient. Every team member must: respect the viewpoints of others on the team, leave their egos at the door, be open-minded to new ideas, participate actively in debate and discussion, and provide challenges from a positive viewpoint.
- Focus on the outcome is the third important ingredient. Powerful team members know that their success comes from the team's success in delivering (and maybe even overdelivering) the promised outcomes. Career management processes support the notion that individual career changes wholly acknowledge the team's achievements and the individual's contribution to that team.

Robyn also mentioned some potential problem points to avoid:

- Is the team a "star team" or a "team of stars?" The "I" should not be more evident than the "we" in team members' actions, words, and attitudes.
- Is there mishandling or negligent handling of underperformers such that the load is carried by others without consequence management?
- Is the team marked by groupthink, which fails to stretch innovation and creativity? Are there any signs of a risk averse culture such that the team's progress is adequate but not powerful?

Cynthia Bottrell, a member of the communications team in Accenture's Office of the CEO, underscored the importance of the following:

◆ A clear sense of purpose for the team as a whole, and a clear view of how every individual team member contributes.

◆ An environment where team members can safely debate, critique, and/or question each others' work—before it leaves the confines of the team. Not only can team members learn a lot from one another, but it always makes for a better end product.

Karen Page, who founded and chairs the Harvard Business School (HBS) Network of Women Alumnae in New York City, mentioned the following points:

◆ Ensure the diversity of your team so that a variety of viewpoints are represented. The HBS case study approach is rooted in the belief that leveraging the efforts of a diverse group or team will result in better analyses and conclusions than any one person could arrive at on his or her own. Like an HBS "section," that diversity ideally should include women and men of various ages, races, nationalities, educational backgrounds, and areas of functional expertise.

◆ Place the right people in the right positions on the team where each has a chance to shine and contribute to the team's overall mission and success. Pave the way for different personality types to work together successfully. (Using tools such as the Myers-Briggs Type Indicator, the Enneagram, or the Kolbe Cognitive Index can be valuable in this regard.)

◆ Tap the potential power of that diversity by drawing out the less outspoken or underrepresented members of the team (that is, those who might feel shy in letting their views be known).

◆ Clarify the goals, objectives, and values of the team so that team members can support one another individually while advancing their collective objectives. The welfare of team members should be of concern to all. Danny Meyer, the legendary restaurateur of Manhattan's Union Square Cafe says it best: "We put our guests second. Caring for each other comes first."

Oklahoma Secretary of State **Susan Savage**'s talk on teamwork at a recent national convention of Women in Communications included two points worth closing with:

◆ Don't forget to laugh. It's important to balance work and play.

◆ Remember that "getting to the goal is more important than getting the credit for the goal."

CHAPTER 8 RECAP

LESSON #23: Strategic networking must become a way of life as CEO of You, Inc.

LESSON #24: Be a team player with a "we" attitude instead of a "me" attitude.

LESSON #25: Pay attention to people—they are your most valuable asset.

ACTION ITEMS:

- Join a networking organization that interests you and provides avenues to achieve your goals.

- Go to events with a purpose: to meet new people and to get to know what they do. Get their business cards and jot three memorable comments on the back as well as any related "to do" points. Perhaps send them an e-mail after you get home— just a brief one saying how much you enjoyed meeting them, and send a copy of an article or something that might be helpful to them, based on something they said during your conversation.

- Develop a system to keep track of the people you meet and how to reach them.

- Review the teams of which you are a part, whether as leader or teammate. Are you using your power effectively or letting it go to your head?

REFLECT AND RECORD:

- Developing a strategic network is as easy as going to a party. What experiences (good and bad) have you had with networking? Who is in your strategic network? Where do you want it to take you?

- How do you handle tough situations? How do you treat people on your team? Are you resilient enough to get ahead?

-9-

MONEY MATTERS

"Woman will always be dependent until she holds a purse of her own."

—ELIZABETH CADY STANTON

Part of any CEO's job is to face the numbers, and as CEO of You, Inc. you must take charge of your financial well-being. Have a vision of how you want your financial life to proceed, a team to help you put it in place, and a plan to help you get there.

What Are the Components of Your "Wealth?"

The first question you should ask yourself when planning your financial future may seem obvious, but is actually quite profound: *How important is money to you?* At a glance, most people would agree that money is greatly important. The more one has, the better! After all, it provides the security of a roof over our heads and food on our tables. It allows us to care for loved ones in the way that we see fit and provide for their futures.

All these things may be true, but the issue of personal wealth becomes much more complicated when you contemplate attaining balance in your life. The reason? Making money tends to be the natural enemy of making time. The more time we devote to our careers and the business of making money, the less we seem to have for other pursuits that may be just as important to us: family, friends, and travel, to name a few.

When I asked a friend how he calculated his personal wealth, I found it thought provoking that he didn't quote the usual "assets minus liabilities" formula. Rather, he mentioned an equation that reflected both his financial and philosophical priorities:

> Personal Wealth = Income + Job Recognition + Growth of Skills and Capabilities + Future Opportunities + Life Balance + Fun

When I reflected on this, it struck a chord with me. I realized that the times I had felt most positive about my personal wealth were when I was feeling good about *all* of the factors on the right side of this equation. Money was part of it, yes, but it was the richness of my life in general that made me happy.

At different times, some of these factors will become more important than others because our priorities change over time. The amount of money you make should be based on the components of your life that matter at any given stage.

For instance, when a former colleague of mine became a new father, the importance of life balance was higher for him than ever. He understood this might negatively affect several of the other factors, including his income and possibly even his future career opportunities in the short-term. However, he determined that the trade-offs were worth it, because he'd had a "weekend dad" and was not willing to be one to his own son.

Taking Charge of Your Finances

An important part of your strategy for You, Inc. is to set goals that will support your financial well-being. How much income do you need to live comfortably? What steps do you need to take to earn your ideal income? What percentage do you need to save or invest to build your nest egg? Where should you invest?

Many of us find financial planning an intimidating process. Because of this, specific members of your team will be essential in helping you reach your financial goals. They should include an accountant or tax person, a banker, a financial advisor, an insurance advisor, and a lawyer. These are the people who will be integral in helping you manage the financial aspects of You, Inc. Remember, it's always good to line these people up before you need them—or to at least have trusted recommendations on hand in case you need them.

The way you handle your finances will set a path for your future. This can be a positive or negative experience. Once people create bad financial habits, they seem to have a hard time getting themselves back on track. No savings, bad credit, poor (or no) planning, and risky investments can all haunt you for years.

Once you have a vision for where you would like your finances to be, and once you've consulted your team, you are ready to take steps toward implementing your goals. What are your financial goals for the next six months? Year? Two to three years? I would suggest that you take a conservative approach to your financial goals. This way, you have a chance to overdeliver—and to celebrate!

To manage your money, there are some general rules to follow. Keeping the big picture in mind will make it easier to implement these steps.

Pay Yourself First

The concept of paying yourself first refers to the practice of consistently investing a percentage of your income as you receive it, before you have the temptation of spending it. Consider arranging to have this done automatically (for example, through automatic withholding) before you ever receive your paycheck.

This is a real commitment, but the payoff of regular investing is astounding. Even if it is only $100 per month, you will be surprised how your dollars will add up over time with compound interest. Remember to adjust the amount you have automatically deposited into your savings or investments as your salary increases. The key is to never let this money make its way into your checking account. If you don't see it, you won't spend it.

Another advantage to paying yourself first is your ability to allocate some of it to a "rainy day" fund (for example, for the day your car's transmission gives out and you need to replace it immediately). As a general rule, you should keep three months of living expenses in an easily accessible account (as opposed to a long-term fund or bond), just in case you need it. This is both important to do—to get you through a personal, family, or career emergency—and to maintain. Commit to upholding this financial cushion, and define how it is to be used (perhaps for taking care of an actual emergency) or not used (like paying your credit card bill).

Stay Current

Pay your bills regularly. Remember, if you don't pay off your credit cards every month, you'll pay significant interest rates for the use of the credit card issuers' money. This can be as much as 18 percent or higher—even a bank loan is less than that. In addition, many credit cards charge late fees as well, which is money that could be going into your savings. The result is that everything you bought will cost you more than what you originally paid.

It is also important to have a good understanding of all of your debts, including your mortgage, car loan, and school loans. When you begin to look at this, you might be surprised at what you pay monthly just for the interest on these debts. When you pay off your debt, pay off the smallest item first. That will give you a sense of accomplishment and give you more money to apply to the next one. Note that the minimum payment covers interest and doesn't pay off the principal.

Develop a Budget

Develop a budget, and live on it. It is essential for you to have a budget that supports both your fixed living expenses (including your tax payments) and your discretionary spending, as well as the monies to reduce your debt and pay yourself, or create an emergency fund. Once you have this entire picture and start to compare your monthly actuals with your budget, you will be able to see how good (or not so good) your financial health is. I had a friend who kept track of his family's daily expenses for several months. This gave him an idea of exactly where the family's money was going and where they could cut back. Remember, a budget is not a "diet; " it's a healthy way of living.

Plan for the Future

Create for the future. This may include education for your children, building a reserve to enable you to make a down payment on a house, or putting money away for your retirement. Depending on your age, these events may sound like they are quite a ways off into the future. However, if you begin contributing even a little bit for the future now, you will get in the habit, and the money will have many years to grow into a nice nest egg.

Plan for Retirement

You can't start too soon to plan for your retirement. I didn't think about it until I was forty or so. By that time, I already had fifteen income-producing years behind me, and I hadn't really started to develop a retirement nest egg. Assistance from a financial planner is well worth the time and investment it takes to design a plan that will provide the money necessary for you to retire.

There are many different plans, including those into which your employer makes automatic contributions. Become familiar with your options via your company's HR department or a financial planner, and see which one meets your retirement goals and your monthly investment plans. As your income rises, don't forget to increase your retirement contributions accordingly.

If you are eligible for an IRA, you may be able to contribute as much as $4,000 or more a year. Many people think they can't afford this. However, take a look at your indulgences: Doing without one music CD, one lunch out, one grande latte, or the latest hardcover book until it comes out in paperback could easily add up to $80 or more a week—which would total $4,000 after 50 weeks. If you begin investing $100 biweekly today and earn an average of 8% annually, in 20 years you will have $123,862 available. But if you wait 5 years to start, your account would have only $73,492. That's a $50,000 difference in your account. Over time, compounding of earnings does most of the work for you. My point here is to start contributing something to your retirement as early as you can.

Now that I no longer work for Accenture, my current assets need to support me for (I hope!) as many as 30 years or so. Let's say you need $50,000/year to live on (including taxes, medical, and general living expenses). This needs to be adjusted for inflation, but to have, say, $50,000 in annual net income, you will need $1,000,000 invested with a rate of return of 5%. Don't be daunted by this number. As I mentioned previously, putting away a small portion of each paycheck can really add up.

Estate planning and wills are also areas in which you should educate yourself. Have your lawyer draw up a will, and update it as you increase the size of your estate. A will is necessary to make sure that those you love, and those causes you care most about, will benefit. Also consider creating a living will, which can circumvent difficult decisions on the part of your loved ones. And make sure that someone you trust knows where to find these documents in the event of an emergency.

Implement Your Financial Plan

To implement your financial plan, you will need to make it part of your daily routine. Set up time every month to review your financials. You are the CFO as well as the CEO of You, Inc., and it is now your responsibility to ensure the financial well-being of your company. Set a date in your calendar to enter the data and develop the reports. Companies usually have their monthly financial reports out by the fifth working day of the following month. This way, it provides opportunity to adjust your spending before the next month is past.

In terms of cash flow, the key is to know what your "cash in" is and to strive to have it be greater than your "cash out." This provides you with some fun money as well as contributions to your nest egg.

Where to begin? Start by knowing where you are today and where you want to be in the future, and determine what you need to do to get there:

- ◆ Know how much your net earnings are after deductions for taxes and retirement plans.
- ◆ Determine how much you want to put aside (pay yourself first).
- ◆ Know where your money is going. I have found that the best way to do this is to keep track on a daily basis of all the cash you spend and where it goes. Include the checks you write and online credit card transactions.
- ◆ Estimate the other charges that only come in on a less than monthly basis, such as insurance payments. A percentage of these amounts should be included in your monthly cash needs.
- ◆ Manage your credit card usage. Consider closing the account if you have trouble managing the charges. This is how people get into trouble: spending, charging, then having to pay the high rates of interest when the bill isn't paid off each month.
- ◆ Be honest with all of these calculations. If not, the financial reports will not be accurate and you will be headed for surprises in the future.
- ◆ Remember: ask for advice.

For the Self-Employed

If you are not working for an organization that provides you with regular paychecks and automatically makes deductions on your behalf, you must be extra vigilant about managing your finances. For freelancers, small business owners, and entrepreneurs, there is a price to pay for your independence: a 15% self-employment tax. This, including other taxes and Social Security, needs to be paid quarterly, rather than annually.

If you are your own boss, you probably don't have spare time to spend mulling over your financial situation. In this case, it is imperative that you have trusted team members to help you avoid the financial pitfalls that can bring an independent endeavor to its knees.

Your Annual Financial Review

Take one day a year—perhaps the same day every year—to review your entire financial and estate planning package for You, Inc. This is your time to take stock on an annual basis and determine the things that need to be changed or added (such as beneficiaries, power of attorney, and investment strategy). This annual review may even spur changes to your goals. The review process will provide you with a document (ideally both electronic and paper copies) to review with members of your team to identify changes that you should consider.

Create the Future

Give back to your community. You receive benefits from your community every day. I know you pay taxes that provide many of these benefits, but it is important to remember that there are many services that are not covered, such as the Girl Scouts, the Boys & Girls Clubs, and the United Way agencies. You can make a difference by getting into the habit of contributing even $5 or $10 every month to a cause about which you are passionate. Think of it as giving up a few Starbucks coffee drinks to increase the quality of someone else's life.

The simple truth is it feels good to give back. And there is a supplemental advantage to it. Each time you engage in a philanthropic act, you set an example for those around you—for kids in your community, for your peers and colleagues, and for whomever takes note of your generosity and is inspired to do the same.

★ ★ ★

While planning your financial life, keep in mind the balance you are striving to achieve in your life. Then, acquire a strong, trusted team that can help you plan, organize, and live a rich life on all fronts. You will find that your wealth is worth sharing with others.

CHAPTER 9 RECAP

LESSON #26: Know how important money is to you.
LESSON #27: Your financial team is essential.
LESSON #28: Follow sound financial practices as CFO of You, Inc.

ACTION ITEMS:

- ◆ Create your own "personal wealth" equation, and evaluate it annually.
- ◆ Identify your financial team: accountant, tax advisor, lawyer, etc.
- ◆ Develop your budget, which includes your fixed expenses and other discretionary needs as well as some money to set aside for emergencies. Ensure your budget allows you to "pay yourself first" while staying within your monthly income.
- ◆ Set up a system to create monthly reports of your financial performance with financial software.

◆ Schedule monthly and yearly financial review sessions.

REFLECT AND RECORD:
◆ Identify opportunities to begin your philanthropic activities with either time or resources.
◆ What are your plans for today to create your future security, your wealth?

-10-

SHARE THE WEALTH

*"How wonderful it is that nobody need wait a single moment
before starting to improve the world."*

—ANNE FRANK

Collect the Gold—and Give Some of It to Others

t's important to give forward to others to help them achieve success.
None of us got to where we are alone, and we create the future by creating the next generation of leaders with our support. And, as
women, we have a responsibility to help other women who are coming up behind us. We should open the doors, or drop the ladders, to
bring them along. It is for this reason that I created the Susan Bulkeley
Butler Institute—an organization whose sole purpose is to reach out
to women and help them achieve their dreams.

I believe it's essential to respect women who want power or want to be successful in what they choose to do, and to help them achieve it. They won't replace you and me, but will only make the sum of the parts even greater.

Look at how your organization enhances the development of women. Does it empower (by providing responsibility, career paths, leadership roles, and the freedom to be creative) as well as actually promote women from within? Is your organization one where women and people of diverse backgrounds can be successful? Are diversity and inclusion of people with differences rewarded throughout the organization? If not, what are you doing about it?

Remember, it all starts at the top. The CEO of your company should provide an environment where women can be successful and move into leadership roles. Whether you are that CEO or the CEO of You, Inc., it is essential that you provide an environment to help the women you touch be successful.

Because I was Accenture's first woman professional, I obviously didn't have any women mentors in the company. After this it's-lonely-at-the-top start, I always have felt it important to *give forward* to other women so that they could learn from me and I could help them be successful.

In the early days, there was a lot of curiosity about what a woman partner looked and acted like. For example, was I simply an "Accenture man in a skirt" (to echo a reference to me when I joined the company)? Or was I feminine, with all the feminine traits: someone who liked to be treated as a woman but was more than qualified to do the work?

In the early days, I made myself as accessible as possible to the younger women. I returned every phone call, and I was willing to discuss any issue others wanted to ask. When visiting one of Accenture's offices, I would suggest that I take the women professionals out to lunch. In fact, after one of these get-togethers, one woman called me to say she had just found out that she was pregnant. She wanted to know what she should do. Whom should she tell? Would "they" make her leave? No other woman professional had ever had to bring up the issue of pregnancy or maternity leave in her office, and, as the senior woman in the company, I was the first person to whom she felt comfortable turning to on this subject.

The result of my approach to being a pioneer? I opened doors for women, I mentored them and helped get them promoted, many to partner.

Bring Philanthropy Into Your Life

If you think about your life as a gift, how are you showing your gratitude to others who may not be as fortunate as you are? Many years ago, I was told: "We need to make a difference in our communities for our having been there." It is so easy to make a positive difference in someone else's life. Invest your time with organizations that interest you, such as the Girl Scouts, Junior Achievement, a place of worship, etc. Or, you can share your wealth through the establishment of a $200 award to help someone buy books for college or a $1,000 scholarship. An even simpler form of philanthropy is doing something as undemanding as having a phone conversation or a mentoring session, or assigning someone to work with you on your next project.

Making a difference philanthropically is something that everyone can do. For instance, during the holiday season, I rang the bells at the Salvation Army kettle for a couple of hours with my sister. We both ended up having a wonderful experience. People gave, then thanked us for giving our time for such a good cause! Several people shared stories about why they gave, including a woman whose husband was put up in a Salvation Army shelter when he lost his wallet during World War II. She told us she's given every time she's seen a kettle since then. Others appeared to just want someone to whom to talk. Despite the brisk weather, it warmed our hearts to hear story after story of how many lives have been touched by the Salvation Army.

There are three important ways to bring philanthropy into your life:

1. The first is to have philanthropy be a part of who you are in your daily interactions with everyone you meet. Make every

interaction meaningful—whether an e-mail, a phone call, a thank-you, a smile, or simple eye contact. It could also mean taking a few moments to help someone in need, such as the lady in a wheelchair to whom I offered assistance while she was trying to get across 42nd Street in New York City and who seemed to be having some difficulty, or someone at the grocery who needed help getting the electric cart to work. Everyone has a moment to spare to make a difference.

2. Second, give financial support to a good cause by putting a few dollars "in the kettle," or by writing a check, no matter what size. Every fall, educational institutions hold their annual fund drives, and other not-for-profits complete their year-end campaigns. Funds for these organizations are decreasing or, at best, just keeping up with inflation, so many are having to cut back their services. As many educational and service organizations are dependent on private funding more than ever before, every dollar helps. What's more, your company may even match your donations, so take advantage of it.

3. Third, give your time to volunteer organizations. By doing so, you can leverage your time to benefit a much larger cause. I have been learning more about First Book, which was founded over ten years ago by my friends Liz Arky, Kyle Zimmer, and Peter Gold, and named to *Forbes* magazine's list of 10 Gold Star charities based on its annual survey of 200 nonprofits, also winning a four-star rating from Charity Navigator, an on-line resource for charitable giving.

Other great opportunities for getting involved might be through serving on your local Junior Achievement (JA) board or teaching for JA in the classroom, or volunteering with the Girl Scouts or Boy Scouts, or at your local homeless shelter. Not only are you able to help deliver their services, but you can develop leadership and other skills, as well as network with leaders in your community.

Women's Coming Wealth

In the coming years, women are going to be managing trillions of dollars. In addition to having their own money, many will be inheriting their parents' wealth as well as that of their husbands. According to CDC Vital Statistics, as of 2000, women make up 51% of the U.S. population and have an expected survival rate that is five years higher than men. Those five years may not seem like much, but note the following dramatic example: at least $41 trillion will pass from one generation to the next by 2044. An estimated 85% to 90% of those managing this money will be women (*Millionaires and the Millennium: New Estimates of the Forthcoming Wealth Transfer and the Prospects for a Golden Age of Philanthropy*, Havens, John J. and Schervish, Paul G., Social Research Institute, Boston College, 1999).

Despite these facts, many women have a scarcity mentality and fear that they won't have enough to live on if they give their money away. This is known as the "bag lady syndrome." Even affluent women tend to be reluctant to part with their holdings. A Harris poll in 2000 found that while 30% of the affluent women surveyed said they needed more than $50 million to feel "completely secure," only 4% of equally affluent men agreed.

Men historically have been the ones who have donated the most major gifts, thereby making change happen. What this means is that, by choosing the organizations to which to donate, men have significant influence over schools, social institutions, and philanthropic organizations. Women must match this.

Echoing the strides women have made in the business world, it's now time for women to "step up and step out" in the world of philanthropy. We need to create the "old girls' network" to raise the big bucks, just like the men. I have witnessed the "old boys' network" in action, and it is very impressive. One person has the idea, decides what he's going to contribute, then asks his buddies (mostly other men) to pony up the same funding. For instance, my friend Jim contributed $25,000 a year for three years to Junior Achievement and asked eight to ten of his friends (including one or two women) to match his contribution. In this way, he helped the local board of Junior Achievement reach its goal of raising three years of operating income.

I don't want to only educate women about philanthropy; I also want to create ideas for women to put their name on buildings, with their own money, the same way the men do. One day, I hope there will be a Susan Bulkeley Butler Building somewhere.

Philanthropy is all about making a difference. My friend Carolyn Losos is known for saying, "The world is run by those who show up." Are you showing up to make a difference in your community? Are you doing your share in bringing women along in their careers? We need to do a better job of showing up in order to leave our communities and people better off for our having been there.

★ ★ ★

It can be a great source of joy to make a difference in the lives of those around you. I was inspired by a woman in Eugene, Oregon. Marie Lush gave over a million dollars to the Eugene Hearing and Speech Center—an institution for which she had no personal need. She did not want any credit for her donation. In fact, she kept her identity a secret for a long while. Her motto (which I hope we all will follow) is

"If not by me, by whom?
If not now, when?"

CHAPTER 10 RECAP

LESSON #29: **Give forward to create a better future.**
LESSON #30: **Reach out and help women achieve their dreams.**
LESSON #31: **Integrate philanthropy into your daily life.**

ACTION ITEMS:

- Identify ways you can bring philanthropy into your life. List organizations in which you are interested, and contact them, looking for opportunities.
- Identify women you can "take under your wing." Give them advice, go have a cup of coffee with them, listen to their concerns, and share your stories.

REFLECT AND RECORD:

- Are you giving forward to affect future generations? Which women are you developing into future leaders?
- What are you doing for the people you interact with on a daily basis (even if it's a smile and a positive attitude)?
- Begin to internalize the phrase: "If not by me, by whom? If not now, when?" What are you doing *now*?

-11-

THE LEGACY OF YOU, INC.

"Follow your 'North Star' to create your legacy."

—SUSAN BULKELEY BUTLER

Congratulations! You, Inc. is on its way to becoming a great success now that you are at the helm. As CEO, you have created your vision, built your team, developed your plan, and begun navigating your journey. You are making things happen *for* you rather than letting things happen *to* you.

By this point, you understand how the Make-It-Happen Model makes managing change . . . well, manageable. Whether your goal is to become the first woman president or just to get to the gym, the MIH Model will expedite your achievement. The key is to be proactive and complete each phase of the process. Internalize the process and use it in everything you do. Remember: no one step will work without the others. The synergy between all of them creates a platform for your success.

The goal here is to achieve the life you want and to inspire others along the way.

Stop, Look, and Listen

As you continue on your journey, it is important that you pause every now and then to evaluate how You, Inc. is performing. Of course, you'll receive feedback from your mentors along the way, but they may only be looking at one department of You, Inc. As CEO, only *you* know the whole story: all your dreams, fears, disappointments, successes, and level of happiness at any given time. Take the time to reflect on your journey. Are you on the right track? Do adjustments need to be made? Is there balance? Are you having fun?

Any successful company assesses itself, and You, Inc. should be no different. Your journal will be a helpful tool as you evaluate where you have been and where you are today. As a CEO, you should document your achievements for the year. Think of this as your annual report.

Creating Your Legacy

When you take the time to evaluate yourself as CEO, look at the meaning behind your daily activities. Is your life going in a direction that has importance beyond making money and surviving? I ask you this because it is incredibly easy to get caught up in the day-to-day routines of our lives. Unless we consciously approach our lives thoughtfully and with purpose, we risk simply coasting through our years.

At a women's leadership workshop over ten years ago, one of the exercises was to write our eulogy to document our legacy. Morbid? Not really. As I remember it now, it gave me a sense of direction for my life. In essence, it gave me a "North Star" for my legacy. I have updated

Eulogy for Susan Bulkeley Butler (1943–20XX)

It is unfortunate, but today we are mourning the loss of Susan Bulkeley Butler. She would, however, want us to be celebrating her life here on earth and the legacy that she left behind.

Susan, daughter of Gene and Mary Bulkeley, was the youngest of three children. She grew up with older siblings Nancy and Dick in a small town, Abingdon, Illinois. She would say this was the number one city in Illinois. After a quizzical look, she would add, well it begins with "Ab," so it is at the top of the list! It was a town of about 3,500 people, and most of her Bulkeley relatives lived on the same block. Another interesting tidbit, everyone in the Bulkeley family had a middle name beginning with C. Hers was Carla. She was always proud of it because her father picked it out, and it meant "love."

She graduated from Abingdon high school, went off to attend Purdue University, and had a plan to go to Galesburg, Illinois, and begin her career in the retail industry. However, after her first year at Purdue, she reevaluated her plan, considered other options, and settled on a bachelor of science degree in industrial management.

With guidance from a professor and others, she settled on going to work at Accenture in Chicago, where she learned all there was to know about computers. She was the first professional in the Accenture organization who happened to be a woman, and later became the first woman partner.

During her thirty-six-year career, Susan had many different roles and responsibilities as the organization grew from approximately 460 people worldwide to over 100,000. There are many legacies that she leaves behind, from the very large project with the U.S. Navy to install an aircraft maintenance system; to helping create a line of business, change management; to leading the Philadelphia office to be recognized as making the city a better place; to leading large corporations through change projects that impacted all of their employees; to the Office of the CEO, helping to lead the company in its transition from Andersen Consulting to Accenture.

She was quite the leader. She was a role model, mentor, and developer of people who always cared for those who were around her.

Helping people be all they can be was something that Susan always did, as she learned this early in life from her parents and family: "You can do anything you set your mind to." That is why she started the Institute for the Development of Women Leaders, to help women achieve their dreams. She said she wanted to "impact zillions of women and girls," each in her own way. She also wrote a book of her lessons so that the women coming behind her could learn by reading and not by having to experience everything that she had. "They have too much to learn on their own, so why not pass forward to them what I have learned to be important?" she would say.

In reflecting on her life and her aspirations, Susan published many books and articles not only for women, but also for young girls. And based on the sales, thousands have read Susan's words and received her call to action to "make things happen *for* you, not let things happen *to* you."

Additionally, because of her relentless concern over the number of women in the technology, science, business, and engineering pipeline, we have seen significant growth in their numbers. And in fulfillment of another of Susan's aspirations, we see that academia is a great place for women, as faculty, professors, department heads, deans, and presidents.

Susan broke barriers, spoke out on the benefits of diversity, and was a leader wherever she found herself. She left many legacies around the world and, as for her character, she was a people person, a team player who was creative and accepted change and, in many cases, helped make it happen. She had time for everyone, big or small, and would say to everyone now, "Continue on, go make your dreams come true and help others that follow you. Be a good steward of future generations, and make the world a better place for your having been here. I know that I did."

it here for your benefit in the hope that you write your own and thus create *your* personal North Star.

Let's face it: we only have so much time to accomplish our goals. For this reason, it makes sense that what we achieve be truly important, influential, and lasting. What do you want to leave behind? What will your legacy be? Affecting people's lives in a positive way is, to me, the most enduring way to be remembered.

★ ★ ★

What will be the legacy of You, Inc.? The answer depends on your vision and the steps you take to achieve it. Each day you have the power to make inroads toward reaching your dreams. If they are approached with intelligence, kindness, and strength, I guarantee your legacy will live on.

CHAPTER 11 RECAP

LESSON #32: **Evaluate how well you are doing as CEO of You, Inc.**

ACTION ITEMS:
- Receive input from your family, mentors, team members, etc., on how well you are running You, Inc.
- Write your own eulogy or legacy. File it away with the important papers for You, Inc. Review it periodically, and see how you are doing. Make changes as necessary. This is the ultimate plan for your life.

REFLECT AND RECORD:
- What are the major achievements you would document in your annual report, and how do you need to update your plan for the next year to be successful in your career and with You, Inc.?
- What do you want to be remembered for?

EPILOGUE

An article that I recently read inspired me to include this epilogue. In "Some Parting Advice" (*Utne*, September–October 2005), author Paul O'Donnell discusses the phenomenon of the ethical will. Briefly, an ethical will is a spiritual document that some people write to their loved ones to pass on history, certain values, pieces of knowledge, and stories. It usually contains information that may not have been expressed during an individual's lifetime, but nevertheless is an important legacy to pass on.

I love the idea of the ethical will and hope that, in a similar vein, my parting counsel will leave you feeling inspired and hopeful. As you reflect on what you have read and on the journal you have started, let's review my ten important guidelines for career success:

- Accept the role of CEO of You, Inc.
- Develop your vision, build your team, create your plan, and navigate your journey to achieve your dreams.
- Find mentors—they are essential to your success.
- Create a marketable "product" and "package" for yourself.
- Market yourself every hour of every day in everything you do (and be good at it).
- Develop a strategic network.
- Invest your time (instead of spending it) to achieve your goals.
- Pay attention to people—your success is in their hands.
- Manage your financial life with an eye to your future.
- Make philanthropy a part of your life; it comes back to you tenfold.

For some of you, this book may have been a confirmation of what you are doing right. For others, it has been a "how to" that I hope has built your confidence. For yet another group, it has been a call to action to take charge of your life, with a strategy to make that happen.

I want you to feel empowered, to dream big, to set your goals, and to get to work! Remember, if you only get halfway toward your dream, it is better than staying put. Even if you are on the right track, you will get run over if you just sit there. I don't want you to get run over, so start moving!

Mark today's date on your calendar as the day you were promoted to CEO, and be *bold*, commit yourself to You, Inc., and make your dreams come true. Check out your progress every three, six, or twelve months to see how you are doing. Ultimately, it will become a way of life.

My dream of touching the lives of "zillions of women and girls" is to have each of you affected by what you have read and to take immediate action to make change happen to you.

My parting message is to enjoy your life. You have only one, so remember to "make things happen *for* you, don't let things happen *to* you." You will be an outstanding CEO of You, Inc.

Your Virtual Mentor,

Susan

ACKNOWLEDGMENTS

Acknowledging everyone who has helped me to make this book a reality is a daunting task. When starting down this path, it's easy to worry about leaving someone out. So, right from the beginning, I want to thank everyone who has been by my side at one time or another. You are all very special to me.

There are many to whom I would like to give special acknowledgment for the contribution they have made either to my book or to my life's experiences that underlie this book:

To my extended family, who taught me to dream big and supported me in everything I wanted to do; my parents, who continue to be my guardian angels from afar; and my closest relatives—specifically Dick Bulkeley, Nancy Baldwin, and Jane Eyre McDonald.

To Abingdon, Illinois, the small Midwestern town where I grew up as part of a large family, many of whom lived on the same block, which taught me how to work for what I wanted to achieve; to be community focused; and to care for every member of the community, no matter who they were.

To Accenture for thirty-six years of experiences and friendships that have enabled me to write this book.

To my many mentors who have helped me in so many ways, particularly Carla Paonessa who was there for every major decision and more.

To my friends at Purdue University who reached out to me early in my career and invited me into the Purdue family to make a difference.

To all the people who kept saying to me, "Susan, you need to write your book"—thank you for helping me make it happen.

To all the people in all of my networks—together, we have been able to make the world a better place for our having been here.

To all those people who helped make this book a reality:

Karen Page had a vision for the institute and for Susan Butler as a "virtual mentor" and everything that entails, even before I did. Thank goodness for her endless help in making the Institute for the Development of Women Leaders and this book come alive. Karen has been my partner in helping zillions of women and girls, planting seeds in the next generation of women, and "giving forward" all along the way. Thank you, Karen.

Mike Stadther and everyone from Paribus Publishing Ltd. have been the creators of my wonderful book. Mike was on my team at Andersen Consulting when we were installing an aircraft maintenance system for the U.S. Navy. Now, he influences the publishing industry through his own innovative projects, in addition to this one. I'm fortunate to have everyone at Paribus on my team to bring my manuscript to life and to reach all of my readers. Thanks to Mike Stadther, Helen Demetrios, Lisa Deutsch, Alexia Paul, Anna Christian, and many others behind the scenes. You have all been fabulous to work with.

Professor Duncan McDonald educated me in the process of writing a book, answered all of my questions, improved my writing style, and made sure the content made sense. Thanks for all you gave to help make sure that my book was the best it could possibly be.

"My team" of readers and contributors are an invaluable part of this story. You all gave me the confidence that my lessons were important and worth sharing. Thank you.

All the special people in my personal life have taught me a great deal. I am here today because of you. You are all a part of this book, and I can't thank you enough for what you have done for me.

Finally, to my spiritual partner who is with me all the time and guides my life—thank you.

Susan Bulkeley Butler
Fall 2005